Business School

Unit 6
Management within the organisation

Written by Stuart Munro and Pauline Gleadle

Module Team

Dr Mike Lucas, *B292 Chair & Author*

Professor Jane Frecknall-Hughes, *Professional Certificate in Accounting Chair & Author*

Elizabeth R Porter, *Regional Manager & Author*

Jonathan Winship, *Author*

Stuart Munro, *Author*

Dr Vira Krakhmal, *Author*

Dr Pauline Gleadle, *Author*

Dr Jane Hughes, *Contributor*

Sam Cooper, *Programme Coordinator*

Emir Forken, *Programme Manager*

Dr Lesley Messer, *Head of Curriculum Operations*

Funmi Mapelujo, *Qualifications Manager*

Kelly Dobbs, *Curriculum Assistant*

External Assessor

Professor Stuart Turley, Manchester Business School

Critical Readers

Richard Davies

Dr Jane Hughes

Developmental Testers

Dr Teodora Burnand

Sam Cooper

Diane Jamieson

Sue Winship

Nicole Wright

Production Team

Simon Ashby, *Media Developer*

Martin Brazier, *Media Developer*

Anne Brown, *Media Assistant*

Vicky Eves, *Media Developer*

Diane Hopwood, *Rights Assistant*

Lee Johnson, *Media Project Manager*

Siggy Martin, *Print Buyer*

Kelvin Street, *Library*

Keith Wakeman, *Service Administrator*

The Module Team wishes to acknowledge use of some materials from B680. *The Certificate in Accounting.*

This publication forms part of the Open University module B292 *Management accounting*. Details of this and other Open University modules can be obtained from the Student Registration and Enquiry Service, The Open University, PO Box 197, Milton Keynes MK7 6BJ, United Kingdom (tel. +44 (0)845 300 60 90; email general-enquiries@open.ac.uk).

Alternatively, you may visit the Open University website at www.open.ac.uk where you can learn more about the wide range of modules and packs offered at all levels by The Open University.

To purchase a selection of Open University materials visit www.ouw.co.uk, or contact Open University Worldwide, Walton Hall, Milton Keynes MK7 6AA, United Kingdom for a brochure (tel. +44 (0)1908 858793; fax +44 (0)1908 858787; email ouw-customer-services@open.ac.uk).

The Open University

Walton Hall

Milton Keynes

MK7 6AA

First published 2011. Second edition 2012.

Edited and designed by The Open University.

Typeset in India by OKS Prepress Services, Chennai.

Printed in the United Kingdom by Cambrian Printers, Aberystwyth.

ISBN 978 1780 0 7385 9

2.1

Contents

Introduction

So far in studying B292 *Management accounting* you have focused on the analytical and numerical role of the management accountant. Obviously this is key to the role of a management accountant, but in order to fulfil that role you are likely to need to manage people. In organisations today, be they for profit or not-for-profit, people are seen as a core resource, probably the most important resource that the organisation has. However, it is not just the internal 'human resource' that needs to be managed: there are groups of people, both internal and external to the organisation, who need to be managed in order to obtain the best results for the organisation.

Until the middle of the last century, it was believed that people were born with the skills needed to manage or to lead people. Today it is recognised that, like any other skill, it is possible to define the particular aspects that make a good manager or a good leader and to learn these core skills. As with any other skills, some people will find them easier to learn than others, but everyone can improve his/her ability to manage or lead by studying best practice, and then practising.

This unit is designed to explain the key elements involved in managing people within an organisation, so that you have a framework from which you can develop your own management and leadership skills. It comprises seven sessions, as follows.

Session 1 starts by looking at the history of management theory – the evolution from 'scientific' or 'classical' theory, where people were considered part of a wider industrial machine, to the 'human relations' theory, which recognises that people respond better to careful motivation. Of course, not all styles of management suit every situation and the session ends by looking at how different styles of management might be adapted to meet different needs.

Session 2 aims to increase your understanding of the people (or groups) who have an impact on an organisation. These are called the stakeholder groups. Management needs to identify these stakeholders and know how best to manage their influence. Some approaches to analysing them are explored.

However, the primary focus in this unit remains the people within the organisation. **Session 3** looks at how these people form a collective culture of the organisation. Parallel to the formal organisational structure, an informal organisation develops. Management needs to recognise and learn how to work with this in order to enhance the overall effectiveness of the organisation.

Session 4 moves on to looking at the motivation of employees, starting with an understanding of basic human motivation and building up to how reward systems can be used to enhance motivation and thus organisational efficiency.

Frequently outcomes are achieved by groups of people. A different set of skills is required to build and develop effective groups. **Session 5** explores some of these skills.

Sessions 6 and 7 take the theoretical concepts of how people and groups behave and explore how they can be applied to formal management of the human resource. **Session 6** explores how to develop a training and development plan while **Session 7** looks at the recruitment of new talent into the organisation.

We hope that you enjoy this unit and find it rewarding. Those of you already working in a management role may be able to put some of the material into practice right away, while for others, these skills are something you will need to develop for the future.

Learning aims and outcomes of Unit 6

Upon completion of Unit 6 you are expected to be able to understand and explain:

1   the nature of management and leadership
2   the importance of stakeholders to an organisation and how to recognise and manage their differing claims
3   organisational culture
4   the need to motivate people in an organisation and the link between motivation and reward systems
5   the nature of groups and how to manage group effectiveness
6   training and development within an organisation
7   recruitment and selection within an organisation.

SESSION **1 Management and leadership**

Introduction

Upon completion of Session 1 you are expected to be able to:

- define and differentiate between leadership, management and supervision
- explain the nature of management, including the contribution to understanding management made by some key management theorists, for example, Fayol, Taylor, Mayo, Mintzberg, Fiedler and Drucker
- explain the nature of leadership, again using the work of major theorists.

In many businesses, particularly when they are starting up or are still small organisations, management is not a conscious process. Consider the example of a self-employed plumber who takes on a school leaver. The plumber does not sign up to the OUBS to study management, although he/she would be welcome. Instead, the plumber either has a natural ability to manage or does not. In the past, people with an ability to manage tended to run more successful organisations and so there appeared to be a natural correlation between successful organisations and more capable management. Larger organisations today will often separate the different roles of management, appointing specialists for roles such as **human resource management**, whereas many smaller organisations may retain all management functions in one person. However it is structured, the task of managers is to guide the organisation towards achieving the goals set by the owners or sponsors of the organisation. How do managers undertake this task?

Many concepts of managing an organisation owe a great deal to Adam Smith, following the publication in 1776 of his work *An Enquiry into the Nature and Causes of the Wealth of Nations*, in which he advocated that labour should be specialised, meaning the division of the tasks to be undertaken into small components and requiring individual workers to become proficient in a narrow range of tasks. However, it was not until the early twentieth century that theorists such as Taylor and Fayol developed modern management theory. Once the nature of management started to be better understood (and this is still an on-going process) it became possible to teach the skills needed to practise it.

1.1 What is management?

A simple definition of **management** is that it is the deployment of resources (both human and physical) in a manner designed to achieve a defined objective. However, this is far too simplistic a view to be of much use here. It gives no detail of how management should approach the organisation of the resources or how it should encourage or motivate staff to cooperate. To gain a richer view, some of the main theories of management, which can be grouped into three categories, will be explored. These are as follows.

Classical or scientific management. These theories dissect the role of management into components in an attempt to understand each component better, and, through this approach, make the overall management of the organisation more efficient. The main proponents of these theories were Frederick Taylor and Henri Fayol.

Human relations management. Elton Mayo postulated that excessive micro-management of individuals did not encourage workers to maximise their productivity and that building a sound, professional relationship with them achieved better results.

Functional management. Here theorists such as Henry Mintzberg and Peter Drucker describe management styles in situational settings, ascribing different styles as appropriate to different situations.

1.1.1   Classical and scientific management theories

Frederick Taylor worked in the USA in the early part of the twentieth century during the birth of factory-based mass production. He published *The Principles of Scientific Management* in 1911 and is one of the few writers with an 'ism' named after him. Taylorism is another name for scientific management, an approach to organising work that had a tremendous effect on manufacturing management, most notably in the car industry. The idea was that workers would carry out highly specialised and narrowly focused tasks for which they would be paid piece-work rates. They would therefore be paid for the quantity of work they produced in a specified period of time. The best example of this was in the old-fashioned assembly line method of production – in fact, it is still sometimes called Fordism (after the Ford Motor Company). This system sought to give management a very high level of control over workers.

'We're almost fully automated now.'

Imagine that Taylor was asked to apply his 'scientific' approach to the role of a so-called tea lady or tea boy. In his time, offices did not have coffee machines but people instead enjoyed a fresh cup of tea, or coffee, delivered to their desk on a trolley, by a tea lady or tea boy. Taylor might specify the size of the cups in order to define exactly how many cups of tea came from one teapot. He would specify the most efficient route the tea lady/tea boy should take and the times that they should arrive at each stop-off point from which they delivered the tea. By analysing each step in the process and providing the most efficient tools for completing each step, Taylor believed that the efficiency of the overall organisation would be maximised.

This scientific approach to work in which people are reduced to the status of machines was well regarded by those who emphasised efficiency at all costs, but poorly regarded by those who believed that trust and cooperation between management and workers were vital in organisational life. Nevertheless, it had a very significant influence on the organisation of work for a large part of the twentieth century.

'Scientific management' has a precise meaning and in this exact form is today, thankfully, rarely seen. A more humanistic approach as advocated by Mayo (which is discussed later) has become more prevalent. Nevertheless, aspects of Taylorism do persist and not all of them are bad. Today, management scientists continue to study the processes of production in order to derive the most efficient way of doing things and, indeed, management accountants who employ standard costing systems are separating the costs of each stage of production and each significant component cost, in order better to understand how the costs of the whole product build up. However, implementing the results of this analysis is, hopefully, undertaken with more concern for individuals and how best to motivate them.

Activity 1.1   ....

Fundamental Taylorism is rare today but, as has been said, aspects of scientific management can still be found as part of the management structure in many organisations. Have you worked in, or do you know of, an organisation with a Taylorist approach to work? If so, how did this manifest itself and did it work?

Allow five minutes for this activity.

Feedback   ....

If you have encountered Taylorism, it was, hopefully, in the way in which individual tasks are divided into smaller, easily understood and managed operations. Perhaps in your early career you were asked to enter data into a database without having responsibility for the overall activity. If you understood the overall activity, you may have seen this as a practical division of labour, with a more experienced colleague using your data to complete higher level tasks. This could make sense if the more experienced colleague needed to apply his/her experience to a range of tasks and did not have time to enter data for each of them. However, if you were not aware of the wider objective and had no opportunity to improve your skill and knowledge, you might have found the task demotivating.

Henri Fayol developed the **classical** or **systematic theory of management** at about the same time that Taylor was developing scientific management. Fayol had been a successful manager in a mining company and wanted to codify what it was that made a successful manager, in order to educate new managers. Before Fayol there was little, if any, formal education in management and so the birth of management education can be largely attributed to him.

Fayol considered that management consisted of five functions. This core assumption has been challenged by more recent theorists such as Peter Drucker and Henry Mintzberg (discussed later). Nevertheless, Fayol's five functions of management offer an informative perspective on the nature of management.

Planning
Implies examining the
future, forecasting
and drawing up
plans of action

Controlling
Implies seeing that
everything occurs
in accordance
with policy and
practice

**Functions of
Management**

Organising
Implies building
up the structure,
material and
human resources
of the organisation

Coordinating
Includes bringing
together, unifying and
harmonising activity
and effort

Commanding
Includes maintaining
the required activities
amongst the
personnel

Figure 1 Five functions of management
(Source: adapted from Fayol, 1949)

1.1.2 Human relations management

Not long after Taylor and Fayol, in the 1920s and 1930s, Elton Mayo undertook a series of experiments at the Western Electric's Hawthorne plant, near Chicago. The **Hawthorne experiments** are still influential in management thinking today.

In one series of experiments Mayo divided workers into two groups:

- a control group where he maintained constant levels of lighting
- an experimental group where he varied the light intensity.

Intuitively, you would expect the control group's productivity to remain constant while the experimental group's productivity would vary with the light intensity. It might improve with more light or decrease if the light intensity was too high. Instead, he found that the experimental group's productivity increased notwithstanding the variations in light intensity. Furthermore, the control group also saw improved productivity.

Mayo believed that the improvement was due to someone taking an interest in the workers, that is, someone had sought his/her opinions. Accordingly, this improvement was a result of this group of workers feeling a sense of involvement in their work. This revelation led to the concept of **social man**.

The scientific and classical management theories of Taylor and Fayol were based on the idea of **rational man**, who would respond logically to any changes that management made to his environment. Social man responds to less quantifiable inputs: praise, esteem, enjoyment of the work, friendship with colleagues, etc.

Mayo noted that the experimental group experienced good communication and an enhanced sense of interest in its work. He concluded that work satisfaction was a strong motivator and that work satisfaction was derived, to a large extent, from informal social patterns of work. When the social conditions are right, the role of physical conditions in efficiency is diminished.

Activity 1.2 ....

Draw up a short list of features common to Taylor's scientific management that conflict with Mayo's findings. Do you think that one approach is always better or might the choice of approach need to be dependent on the situation?

Allow about five minutes for this activity.

Feedback ....

You may have considered the following features which epitomise the differences between Taylor and Mayo.

Key features of Taylorism	Mayo's contrast
Rational man: people will respond to the logic of efficient 'scientific' production.	Social man: efficiency is achieved through motivating people.
Task management: improving efficiency by sub-dividing and closely managing each task.	People management: people work harder when management pays attention to their needs and desires.
Time management: by designing the quickest way to achieve each sub-task overall efficiency is enhanced.	Mayo again argued that the concepts of 'social man' and 'people management' achieve higher efficiency than micro-task and time management.

As regards the choice of approach, you may have argued that Mayo's would always be the most efficient and most humane. Alternatively, you may have argued that, where detailed highly technical work is performed, Taylorism may prove to be more efficient, particularly if it is possible to sub-divide tasks into smaller units which can be monitored in detail.

1.1.3 Management functions

Henry Mintzberg was first mentioned in Unit 1 where his input into the understanding of organisational structures was discussed. During the 1970s, Mintzberg also undertook research into actual management behaviours, observing the work of chief executives in five organisations. He observed that, in reality, managers do not devote much time to thoughtful analysis but instead are highly active. Their day is a series of brief actions skipping from one topic to another with little continuity.

Mintzberg (1980) identified six characteristics common to these managers, in that they:

- all suffered from large workloads and tight time pressures
- spent only a short time on each activity in a fragmented way
- chose action over paperwork
- preferred meetings (face to face or telephone) to reading reports

At first sight, these findings about the work of chief executives are rather surprising. Before reading this, did you think that chief executives would be engaged more in 'thinking', rather than in 'action', as identified by Mintzberg?

- concentrated relationship development on subordinates and 'outsiders', with less attention paid to superiors
- while initiating many decisions, had limited direct involvement in the execution of work.

Despite this seemingly chaotic approach to managing, Mintzberg did identify ten key roles required of managers, as shown below.

Interpersonal		
	1. **The Figurehead**	Performs symbolic duties as the head of the organisation
	2. **The Leader**	Fosters a work atmosphere that encourages and motivates others
	3. **The Liaison**	Acts as a conduit to external organisations through a network of contacts

Informational		
	4. **The Monitor**	Collects and reviews information from internal and external sources
	5. **The Disseminator**	Passes on relevant factual and value-based information to subordinates
	6. **The Spokesperson**	Informs outsiders of the enterprise on policies and performance

Decisional		
	7. **The Entrepreneur**	Develops and adapts the organisation to meet challenges
	8. **The Disturbance Handler**	Handles unexpected challenges
	9. **The Resource Allocator**	Allocates resources to organisational operations
	10. **The Negotiator**	Manages the relationship with outside individuals and organisations

Figure 2 Ten roles of management
(Source: adapted from Mintzberg, 1980, pp. 166–170)

Mintzberg grouped these into three blocks based on where managers derived their authority for the tasks:

- **interpersonal authority**, derived from the formal position within the organisational structure
- **informational authority**, derived from access to contacts within and outside of the organisation
- **decisional authority**, where interpersonal and informational authority combine to empower managers to take decisions.

All these roles are interdependent in that good decisions cannot be made without good information and the decisions would probably not be well implemented and monitored without good interpersonal roles. In practice, managers would alternate between these roles as required. Mintzberg further configured these roles into those that frequently came together when managers performed certain natural groupings of roles. These natural groupings are shown in Figure 3.

Peter Drucker (1977) took a different approach from Mintzberg. Instead of looking at what managers actually did, he suggested that managers should be attempting to align the results of their department with the objectives of the organisation. To achieve this, he argued that there were three primary tasks:

- *managing a business* to achieve economic success through the creation of customers and through innovation

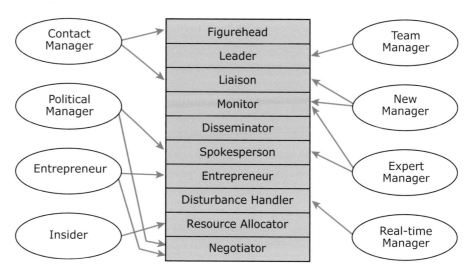

Figure 3 Management role configuration
(Source: Mintzberg, 1980, adapted from www.provenmodels.com/88/
ten-managerial-roles/mintzberg,-henry)

- *managing the managers*, namely, managing by objectives, structuring the organisation and the management roles within it, creating the next managers and developing an appropriate culture

- *managing workers and work*, which recognises that people are the only one true resource of an organisation. To make work and workers productive, managers must design the work so that it is organised logically. It must also meet the physiological and psychological needs of the worker.

Drucker advocated defining corporate objectives at board level and then cascading these down to departments and individuals. If the board set the right 'top level' objectives, the resultant cascade of objectives was a powerful way for the board to manage senior managers, for the senior managers to manage middle managers and so on.

To turn this concept into a practical methodology for management, Drucker considered what the main functions of a manager should be in order to achieve the objective. He listed five things that managers need to do well:

- set objectives

- organise

- motivate and communicate

- measure results

- develop people (including oneself).

Activity 1.3 ....

Map each of Drucker's functions on to Mintzberg's roles. Are any of Drucker's functions not fully covered by Mintzberg's work?

Spend about five minutes on this activity.

Feedback ....

Unlike the earlier scientific and classical theories, Drucker does specifically identify motivation and communication, although he may not give it as much prominence as Mayo. Mintzberg, on the other hand, appears to under-emphasise the development of staff, unless it is included in the team manager role. As you will see when motivation and group development are discussed, developing staff is now recognised as a critical role for managers.

You now have a set of models describing management. To a degree, Drucker combines both the classical approach – managing by objectives – and the humanistic approach with the 'motivate and communicate' and 'develop people' functions. This is getting closer to the complex management roles required in organisations today. However, it does little to explain how an organisation is driven forward into new environments and situations. All organisations need to change at times and, surely, managing this is also a role of managers. In reality, most writers on the subject identify a different set of skills for managing change and attribute that to leadership.

1.2 Leadership

Activity 1.4 ....

Are managers also leaders? Take a few moments to list three or four people you consider to be, or to have been, great leaders.

Allow five minutes for this activity.

Feedback ....

Your list will no doubt be slightly different from ours, but it is likely to have many similarities. There are likely to be some military leaders – Napoleon and Alexander the Great, perhaps. There will probably be some politicians – Churchill and de Gaulle may be examples. There are many more, some of whom you may not like, but whose leadership skills you nevertheless recognise. They all have one thing in common: they were placed in a position where they had to lead large numbers of people. They were 'up to the task', but are there others who could also be great leaders but have not been given the opportunity to prove it?

Now consider your list and ask, were they good (meaning 'competent') managers? The answer is, 'probably'. Most management theorists argue that there is a distinction between the roles of managers and leaders but accept that there is a degree of overlap between the two (with the notable exception of John Kotter whose views are discussed later). Truly good leaders have to be able to perform some of the roles of management just as good managers have to display some degree of leadership. These are two overlapping but not identical skill sets. The differences are subtle, but leaders have a vision of where they want to go, and take others along with them, while managers focus on the mechanics of the journey, ensuring that people get there efficiently.

1.2.1   The functions of leadership

What is leadership? Looking at the functions of leadership will help to answer this question.

John Kotter is a well known writer on leadership.

John Kotter's (1988) work on leadership stems from the 1980s in the USA. He strongly defended the view that management and leadership are different functions and that managers do not undertake leadership functions. He argued instead that managers are responsible for ensuring order and efficiency in the organisation – while leaders are responsible for having a vision of the future and then forcing the organisation to adapt to that vision – they 'cope with change'. For managers to force through change would endanger the maintenance of order and efficiency.

This is a helpful distinction. The world is changing at an increasing pace. Many companies that a generation ago were considered the bedrock of a country's infrastructure have disappeared. For example, ICI, once seen as the flagship firm of the chemical industry in the United Kingdom, shrank in size until the remnants were purchased by other companies. Meanwhile, many of the new giants operate in sectors not even dreamed of a generation ago – Google, for example. Managers are charged with running the business, as it is an essential role. However, if they focus on this, there must be someone else who focuses on managing the dynamics of change, Kotter claims. This is the role of leaders.

Do you agree that managers should not lead? You may think that this is a little too polarised a view, but many writers on leadership discuss the function of managing change.

1.2.2 Leadership qualities

While the majority of writing on the subject supports Kotter's view of the distinct functions for management and leadership, not everyone sees them as mutually exclusive. Warren Bennis (1998, p. 40) states that, while managers look at near term issues, maintaining systems and ensuring that they 'do things right', leaders are focused on people by nature, meaning that they are more interested in people and personal relationships than in tasks. They tend to be innovators or drivers of change and they create an atmosphere of trust. They 'do the right thing'. In this context, Drucker has drawn a distinction between effectiveness (doing the right thing) and efficiency (doing things right), a distinction you may find helpful.

Interestingly, Bennis considers that the leadership role is a shared one, supporting the view that managers adopt leadership roles when the situation requires it. Indeed, he considered that leadership can be viewed as the use of skills that most of us have, but few use.

In researching the qualities that leaders had in order to persuade others to follow them, Bennis identified four themes:

- *attention*: leaders need to provide focus towards a strong vision, in order to gain the attention of their followers
- *meaning*: leaders' communication needs to be infectious, imparting meaning and enthusiasm
- *trust*: leaders have integrity and consistency in the application of the core values of the organisation
- *self*: they are aware of their own strengths and weaknesses.

Bennis's qualities evidently do offer some insight into what makes a good leader, but this list is probably not complete. Other researchers have produced more extensive lists of traits common to good leaders, but perhaps a more interesting direction is to look at what good leaders actually do.

Like Kotter, Ron Heifetz also believes that a leader's role is to facilitate change. However, Heifetz (1994) argues that it is not always the person with organisational power who leads individuals, but suggests that a leader may emerge from the process. The concept of adaptive leadership assumes that leaders differentiate between technical problems and adaptive problems. Technical problems are issues that the current organisation is fully capable of managing, whereas adaptive problems require the organisation to change and need a new set of functions, or new processes. According to Heifetz and Laurie (1997, pp. 125–29), to overcome these adaptive problems, leaders must act as outlined below.

Get on the balcony. They should stand back from the problem and take a careful look at all of the issues; reflect on the individuals and groups involved; and build a solid foundation of people to tackle the problem.

Identify the adaptive challenge. They need to recognise exactly what the challenge to the organisation is and that it exists.

Regulate distress. They must ensure that a 'holding environment' (p. 127) exists to nurture change and control its pace; carefully establish the direction; and remain confident in order to calm frustration and anxiety in others.

Maintain disciplined attention. They should keep all of the team together despite their differing approaches to change; keep them focused on the objectives; consider who will be supportive of the changes and who will oppose them; build a support base and try to win over any people who are undecided; and remember that change is threatening and that concern can drive much of the resistance.

Give work back to the people. They should let subordinates use their skills, which will assist the team to function and to develop confidence in the change.

Protect voices of leadership below. They should invite input from subordinates, encourage them to take responsibility and drive change.

Heifetz believes leadership to be a social process and, as you can see, that all the functions of adaptive leadership involve social processes. However, Robert Blake and Jane Mouton (1964) make a stronger distinction between leaders focusing on people as a means of achieving an organisation's objectives, and leaders focusing on the objectives themselves.

1.2.3 Behavioural styles of leadership

From research undertaken in the 1960s, Blake and Mouton believed that there were two key behavioural dimensions:

- *a concern for people*, meaning the value that a leader places on the individual, his/her development and interests, when leading a task
- *a concern for production*, meaning the degree to which a leader values objectives and efficiency when leading a task.

Blake and Mouton did not see these as mutually exclusive, but rather that each existed within its own continuum, and to describe this they plotted the dimensions on a grid, as shown in Figure 4.

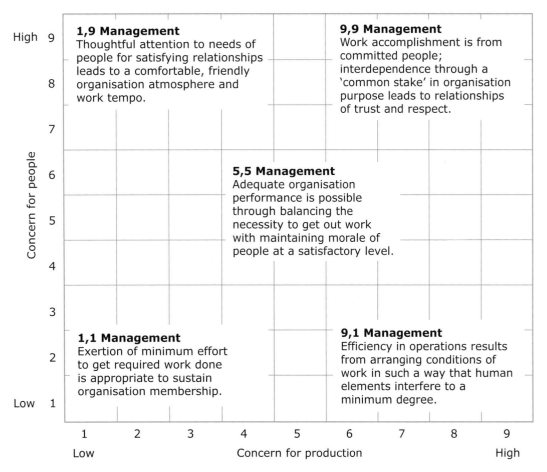

Figure 4   Blake and Mouton's managerial grid
(Source: Blake and Mouton, 1964, p. 10)

Plotting the behaviours of any leader on this grid produces five styles. Of course, no leader is likely to fit perfectly into any one style but will be located somewhere along the continuum. Nevertheless, Blake and Mouton's work produces some useful focal points to help in understanding the nature of leadership.

A leader with high concern for people but low concern for production (point 1,9 on the grid) believes that as long as the team members are happy, they will meet the objectives. While this might be an enjoyable team to work in, it can lack direction.

Conversely, a leader with high concern for the production and low concern for people (point 9,1 on the grid) drives the team hard, with exacting rules and punishment for non-achievement. Team members might become demotivated under such conditions with a detrimental impact on the quality of the results.

A leader who has low concern for both production and people (point 1,1 on the grid) is likely to develop a team with no direction or motivation. Disorganisation and disharmony would be rife, with low achievement likely.

It might seem that balancing both concern for people and concern for production (point 5,5 on the grid) produces the best balance, but Blake and Mouton believed that this approach compromised on both dimensions, with the likelihood of achieving only average results.

The favoured style is to be found at point 9,9 on the grid where the needs of production are stressed but the workforce is involved in understanding the aims and taken along, led by the leader.

Tannanbaum and Schmidt (1958) also looked at leadership styles but their dimensions consist of the degree to which leaders consult others and the degree to which they dictate action.

Autocratic leaders *tell*, or dictate instructions. This can achieve quick results when essential, but it does not build commitment from the rest of the team. Other leaders *sell* or persuade the team to carry out instructions. This encourages initiative and builds commitment. When a leader *consults*, he/she listens to what subordinates have to offer, but still makes a clear decision on what action should be taken. Employees are motivated and develop, but this approach lacks the immediacy of 'telling' them what to do. Where a leader *joins*, he/she undertakes a democratic process which is very rewarding for participants and highly motivating, but can result in very slow decision making.

Studies have found that subordinates valued consistency in the application of styles, but when given consistency, preferred the consulting style of leadership although they associated a selling style more with being led.

Activity 1.5

Consider a leader in the organisation that you work for, or an organisation that you know well. Where does he/she fit on the Blake and Mouton grid? Do the styles described by Tannanbaum and Schmidt provide any more insight into that leader's style?

Spend about five minutes on this activity.

Feedback

Did you find that the leaders you know do not behave consistently? While a step forward from a basic listing of leadership traits, this analysis of behavioural styles still fails to describe completely the styles of good leaders. Good leaders seem to be able to nurture subordinates when they have the time, but can adopt a more autocratic style when needed, for example, when time is short. Fred Fiedler is probably the best known proponent of this contingency theory of leadership.

1.2.4   Contingency theory

The behavioural approach to leadership alludes to the idea that different styles of leadership suit different circumstances, but does not develop this theme. Fred Fiedler (1967, p. 15) developed this as **contingency theory**. Imagine that you are running a small manufacturing workshop in a local town making specialised tools. When the economy is performing well, there is likely to be plenty of demand for your tools and you may consider opening a new factory somewhere else in the UK to better capture a growing industry base in that region. For a while it may be appropriate to show more concern for people than for production, as you want to develop managers to run the new factory. Then the situation changes: the economy goes into recession and the business is fighting for orders, with no hope of opening a new factory in the foreseeable future. If it is a case of getting an order out on time to get paid or run out of cash, you would probably become more production-oriented. Your team would understand this, and adjust with you. It can be sensible to adjust your style as the situation demands.

Here, 'contingency' refers to the view that the effectiveness of a particular strategy, structure or management style, for example, depends on the presence or absence of other factors.

Fiedler developed the **least preferred co-worker theory** (Fielder, 1967, p. 13). This concept does not suggest that managers can change their style, but it does suggest that different managers have different styles, and that different managers fare better in different situations. The model looks at the relationship between leadership style and the effectiveness of that leadership and concludes that there is no one leadership style that is ideal for all situations.

Fiedler asked leaders to select, from people they had worked with, the person they would least want to work with again. The leader then ranked this 'least preferred co-worker' on a series of scales ranging between positives (such as helpful, supportive and trustworthy) to negative (unhelpful, hostile and untrustworthy). The scoring was used to identify the styles of the leaders. High scores meant that even the least preferred co-worker could be seen as reasonably trustworthy, etc., indicating that the leader was empathetic with his team, or was concerned for people. Conversely, a low score correlated to concern for the task.

Fiedler concluded that there were two extremes of leadership style, as described below.

- **Psychologically distant managers**: task oriented managers who maintain their distance from subordinates. These managers prefer structured relationships with staff, and formal, rather than informal, communication methods.

- **Psychologically close managers**: people-oriented managers who are more concerned with maintaining good relationships with subordinates. They prefer informal communication over formal, structured meetings.

Fiedler then related his findings on leaders to the nature of tasks at which teams led by that leader were most likely to be effective. He rated these situations according to how favourable they seemed.

A highly favourable situation would involve:

- a highly structured task with clear rules and procedures for completing the task
- the team members acknowledging the leader's authority to evaluate their performance and to reward good performance or punish poor performance
- the leader having a strong working relationship with the team members.

A highly unfavourable situation would be the reverse: poor structure, members unclear about the leader's authority to reward or punish them and a poor working relationship between the leader and the team (see Figure 5).

Task oriented leader, low LPC score	Relationship oriented leader, high LPC score	Task oriented leader, low LPC score

Highly favourable situation   Situational favourableness   Highly unfavourable situation

Figure 5 Least preferred co-worker (LPC)
(Source: adapted from Fiedler, 1967, p. 14)

What Fiedler discovered is that at either extreme the teams performed better with a task-oriented leader. Where the situation was neither extremely favourable nor unfavourable, teams would benefit from a relationship-oriented leader.

John Adair (1973) argued for an adaptive or contingent approach to leadership. He focused on how a leader can manage his/her people to achieve the organisation's objectives. He identified three overlapping areas of focus, as shown in Figure 6.

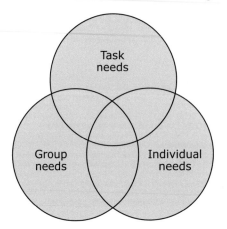

Figure 6 Action centred leadership
(Source: Adair, 1973, p. 115)

Task needs. Achieving the team goal.

Group needs. Setting team standards and encouraging its development, clarifying its role and managing the interaction of individuals within the team.

Individual needs. Guiding, evaluating and providing feedback, and additionally, motivating, encouraging, training and developing.

The activities that leaders are required to perform in addressing these needs are:

- defining the task
- planning
- briefing
- controlling
- evaluating
- motivating
- organising
- setting an example.

The specific activities employed will depend on the needs of each area so that leaders will need to adapt their use of activities according to their focus of attention, as well as the specific need of that area. Adair argued that all areas need to be addressed, but that individual areas may provide the dominant need at any particular time.

Finally, Adair looked at the team, arguing that a team must be built and developed so that it is increasingly effective. Team and group building is discussed in Session 5.

Heifetz also provides some valuable insight into the separation of leadership and the exercise of the authority given to an individual by his/her position in the organisation. You saw how leaders meet adaptive challenges through the performance of leadership processes. It is likely that an individual will not be an ideal leader for all adaptive challenges and that different 'informal' leaders will emerge.

1.3 Supervision

Section 1.2 argued that leadership is associated with management. Leadership and management overlap in terms of functions although there are some differences. Similarly, supervision is also strongly associated with management. However, supervision can be viewed as a junior form of management with some restricted role functions. Supervision is a low level management role, not in the sense that the supervisor is junior (although that is commonly the case), but in the sense that the management skills applied in supervision are not as important a component of the supervisor's overall role compared with a manager's.

For example, if a department store takes on some new part time staff, it may ask experienced section managers to look after the new members of staff and show them how to do the work. They will supervise them, including showing them how to manage inventory rotation, re-stocking of the displays and how to take payment for goods purchased. Such a manager will be the first person the part time staff will talk to if they have a problem. The supervisor manages this daily interface but has limited strategic influence on the staff; he/she does not set company policy about the employment of part time staff nor does he/she select individuals for promotion.

Another example might reveal that a supervisor is not always a junior employee, but rather an employee undertaking a limited management function. A large public company may employ an economist. The economist will be highly trained, may have worked in a number of roles as an economist and be well remunerated. However, his/her management function may be limited. If the company now takes on a junior to 'number crunch', the economist may guide the junior, showing the new recruit how to do the job. The economist will then 'supervise' the new person but not 'manage' that junior's overall role within the organisation.

There are therefore two key characteristics of a supervisor:

- *operational*: he/she performs an operational rather than a strategic or tactical management function in the organisation
- *functional manager*: he/she provides the day to day management contact for staff under his/her supervision, communicating both upwards and downwards within the organisation.

Summary

There are many theories surrounding management and leadership and this session covers quite a number of them. Reviewing these should enable you to answer the question posed in Section 1.1: 'What is management?'

Management is answerable to the owners or sponsors of an organisation for its primary responsibility – achievement of an organisation's goals. To achieve this, managers must organise the workforce and the resources: they need to monitor the performance of the workforce and correct any deviation from the desired course. They must also ensure that the work is carried out in a manner aligned with corporate values, ethics and principles.

From your studies of some of the leading theorists, you should also appreciate how managers manage. Taylor and Fayol described a very rigid classical or scientific approach, some aspects of which persist today. However, it was Mayo who developed the concept of 'social man' where the quality of the relationship with the workforce largely supplanted the earlier formulaic approach as the best way of enhancing productivity. Of course, not all situations benefit from the same style of management and so the functions or roles of managers were explored. It was recognised that the best managers adapt their role to suit the situation.

In the second part of this session you looked at leadership. Although Kotter considered the role of a leader to be distinct from that of a manager, most theorists see them as complementary functions often exercised by the same individuals. Leadership is often associated with driving change and inspiring performance and, for a long time, was perceived as something with which you were born, something you could not learn. The section considered how leaders operate by exploring the work of people like Blake and Mouton. There are different styles of leadership. Tannanbaum and Schmidt provide four useful styles to consider: selling, telling, consulting and joining. However, it is perhaps the contingent theories of leadership that are the most informative. Fiedler described different leadership styles and argued that they are appropriate in different situations. However, Adair went further in suggesting that the best leaders adapt their style to meet the needs of different centres of focus.

SESSION 2 Stakeholders and stakeholder claims

Introduction

Upon completion of Session 2 you are expected to be able to:

- identify the main stakeholder groups affected by an organisation
- identify the disparate objectives of each stakeholder group and how they may conflict
- understand the dimensions of power wielded by each stakeholder group
- explain the interaction of each stakeholder group with other stakeholder groups.

You saw in Unit 1 that commercial organisations exist primarily to make profit and so enhance the wealth of their owners. Not-for-profit organisations and cooperative firms/social enterprises have long been seen as aiming to benefit a broader group of interested parties. While it remains the primary purpose of commercial organisations to generate wealth for their owners, in this session you will see how the broader stakeholder groups are being increasingly recognised as important constituents in shaping strategy and managing all types of organisation.

2.1 What is a stakeholder?

Stakeholders have existed since business organisations were first formed but it is only comparatively recently that a wide range of stakeholders has been recognised as being important in influencing the strategy and management of an organisation.

No more persuasive argument can be found in support of the importance of stakeholder influence than in the demise of organisations that failed to take full account of all stakeholders. The on-going post mortem into the demise of Enron has revealed that most stakeholders (including shareholders) were poorly informed about the true actions and performance of Enron. Had all stakeholder groups been appropriately informed and had they exercised their right and obligation to influence management, it is argued that many of Enron's excesses may have been avoided.

Who are these groups that can yield influence over an organisation and where does their power come from?

Activity 2.1 ....

Read the following *Financial Times* article entitled 'Which stakeholder should get priority?' and list the three main stakeholder groups discussed.

How does each of these exert pressure on the management of the company?

Spend about ten minutes on this activity.

Which stakeholder should get priority?

By Luke Johnson

Who should come first in a business: customers, shareholders or staff? This question is the corporate version of the parlour game I outlined last week concerning power, money and reputation – who wins the triangular struggle for priority?

At Johnson & Johnson, the fabulously successful healthcare business, the answer is, apparently, customers, customers, and customers. Serving them well over many decades has clearly worked for the other stakeholders – its shares have performed outstandingly in the long run, while its staff have enjoyed the security of working at an expanding and reputable company.

However, this formula does not necessarily apply in other industries. For example, supermarket suppliers are notoriously bullied by their customers, the retailers, and they tend to make low margins. I recently met the owner of one supplier who refuses to work much for any British grocer save Waitrose, because the others demand such onerous terms. It is surely no coincidence that Waitrose is part of the John Lewis Partnership, where the owners are also the staff – so there are only two elements in the bargain, rather than three.

At the other extreme, a friend told me that when he worked at the British conglomerate Hanson Trust, its overriding motto was shareholders first, second and third. All other interests were subordinated to the demands of the providers of capital: an increasing share price, and a progressive dividend policy. This philosophy guided the group in an acquisition spree over two decades. But eventually the stock rating declined, and takeover targets resisted its entreaties. Without mergers to enhance earnings, Hanson's raison d'être dissipated, and it was broken up.

Meanwhile, British Airways is another category altogether. There, thanks to power-crazed unions and a defined benefit pension scheme, the hierarchy is clearly staff, staff, staff. The entire undertaking has become but a device to keep the staff pension plan solvent. The flight crew's aborted strike was a self-destructive attempt to defend partisan interests at the expense of everyone else – even if it meant obliterating the entire enterprise. It is useful to know how little BA staff thinks of the customers who provide their revenue. There can be no question that a bankruptcy of BA would actually be a rational outcome for the travelling public. It would permit the business to shed legacy liabilities and invest for the future as a competitive airline – rather than cling on, ever weaker, as a hostage to its past as a state monopoly.

There is an argument that for a number of financial services businesses, such as RBS and Merrill Lynch, at least some of the staff and management must have similarly concluded that the whole operation was designed exclusively to enrich them: that heritage, stockholders, customers and society could go to hell. No wonder both banks had to be rescued.

Great leaders are brilliant jugglers of these competing interests. They judge value and adjust pricing so as to offer attractive goods at a bearable margin. In doing so, they generate sufficient surplus to fund investment and reward loyal owners. And they treat staff well to motivate them to work hard and deliver excellent service. Thus a virtuous, reinforcing cycle proceeds for ably managed concerns.

The ideal arrangement is for the three constituents to cooperate for their mutual benefit. Such profitable and harmonious partnerships are very hard to maintain, since each party tends to expect a growing slice – and the pie is shrinking almost everywhere. But, as Samuel Goldwyn said: 'Ninety per cent of the art of living consists of getting on with people one cannot stand'. It is a matter of compromise and balance.

In spite of popular suspicion, no company – save a monopoly – survives for long if it consistently treats customers badly, for at its heart every organisation relies on repeat business. This is the profound truth in favour of choice and the market. And no enterprise can function without its people or funding. Thomas Macaulay, the historian, put it well: 'It is evident that many great and useful objects can be attained in this world only by cooperation'.

(Source: *Financial Times*, 23 December 2009)

Feedback ....

While any definition of a stakeholder must include the owners of commercial organisations, it is evident that a much wider definition is required. Three primary groupings which can be identified from the article are:

- customers, who are external
- shareholders, classed as external in Activity 2.2, but often regarded as internal
- staff (internal).

Customers can exert pressure on a company, for example, by choosing to fly with a competitor and, during a prolonged period of strike action, are likely to choose to do so. Shareholders can exert influence more directly by voting out the company's executive directors at the next shareholders' meeting. Before that meeting they can exert pressure through lobbying the management and, although it is principally the institutional shareholders who have an opportunity to do this, smaller shareholders can exert influence through shareholder groups. Staff, as seen in the example, can withdraw labour in order to exert influence.

A definition of a stakeholder is any individual, group or organisation whose objectives are affected by the actions of an organisation and who, in turn, has an impact on the strategy, objectives and management of that organisation.

The obvious stakeholders are the people who own the business, the shareholders, and the people who work there. However, a much wider group of stakeholders can have an impact on the strategy of an organisation. There are two broad groupings:

(i) **internal stakeholders** – who are individuals, groups or organisations that work for or manage the organisation

(ii) **external stakeholders** – of which there are two sub-divisions: those who have an operational or contractual relationship (sometimes referred to as 'connected' stakeholders) and those who do not.

Activity 2.2 ....

Using the FT article, develop a list of all the stakeholders that you can think of who would be involved with British Airways. Briefly explain why they would be interested and from where they get their power to influence British Airways (though, of course, they may not have any power). Try this on your own before looking at the feedback.

Allow ten minutes for this activity.

Feedback ....

Here is our list – although you may have thought of more.

Internal stakeholders	Interest	Power to
Cabin crew	Career, pay	Withdraw labour
Ground crew	Pay	Satisfy customers
Pilots	Status	Affect operational efficiency
Management	Security	Affect decision making

External stakeholders marked (c) are considered connected.

External stakeholders	Interest	Power to
Shareholders (c)	Stability of BA Profitability of BA Value of shareholding Dividend stream	Sell shares, depress share price Vote management board out of office Control (if they exercise it) of remuneration committee
Lenders (banks, bond-holders) (c)	Stability of BA Safety of lending Payment of interest and principal	Reduction or withdrawal of future funding Price of future finance
Suppliers (c)	Stability of BA Ability to pay BA's growth	Refusal to supply
Customers (c)	Quality of service Price	Switch airlines
Unions	Interest of employee groups	Increased pressure by employees acting as a group
Government	Air safety Taxes Interest in infrastructure	Legislation and regulation Tax rates Tax breaks
Local population (near to airports)	Noise levels	Limited Pressure groups Enlist other stakeholders Government
Environmentalists	Pollution levels	Limited Pressure groups who can enlist other stakeholders, such as Government

Management will have a second set of interests aligned with those of the owners.

In the feedback for Activity 2.2, you will notice that four employee groups are listed. This is because they are likely to have different objectives. Indeed, some cabin crew members will have different objectives from others. Just because stakeholders are grouped together, perhaps for convenience, it does not mean that they always want the same things. This theme will be revisited later.

Activity 2.3   ....

Consider an organisation with which you are familiar. This may be the organisation for which you work or one where you are a non-employee stakeholder. Identify the various stakeholders and consider what their objectives are. What is it that they want from the organisation?

Allow about ten minutes for this activity.

Feedback   ....

It is likely that you found that the objectives of some stakeholders conflict with others. You may, for example, see a need for management to reduce the size of the workforce in order to meet an objective of the owners but, of course, this conflicts with the objective of the workers who want stable employment. Understanding the relative power of each stakeholder will assist management in balancing these differing objectives.

2.2 Evaluating and managing disparate stakeholder objectives

The management of an organisation needs to be able to evaluate the relative influence that each stakeholder can wield in order to devise a strategy that best manages the overall stakeholder environment. Johnson et al. (2005) adapt a framework from Mendelow (1991) which can be useful in evaluating the relative power of each stakeholder. This adapted framework is shown in Figure 7.

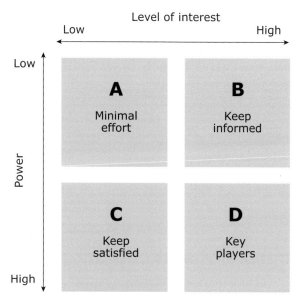

Figure 7 Stakeholder mapping
(Source: adapted from Johnson et al., 2005, p. 182)

Johnson et al. suggest that stakeholders with a high level of interest in impressing their expectations on the organisation's purpose and who also enjoy a high level of power (quadrant D – key players) have the strongest influence on organisational strategy. They argue that quadrant C is often the most problematic. Stakeholders in this quadrant are normally passive, for example, large institutional shareholders in a major company, but if they become unhappy with a strategy, they can suddenly become very troublesome and reposition themselves into quadrant D. It is important therefore to keep them satisfied.

Stakeholders with a high interest but low power (quadrant B) also have an important role to play. One particular group that often falls into this quadrant would be environmental activists. Take, for example, a supermarket chain: activists may promote environmentally sound sourcing of food, but their direct influence on the company may be limited. Nevertheless, many supermarkets pay attention to this group of stakeholders because their activities influence other stakeholders. They may influence the buying habits of customers or, perhaps, even of the otherwise passive institutional stakeholders who wish to enhance their reputation by supporting an environmental movement. Johnson et al. suggest that activists be 'kept informed' so that they do not exert a negative influence on other stakeholders.

This leaves stakeholders with low interest and minimal influence (quadrant A), who require minimal effort to maintain. This group might include residents near a supermarket who, unless they become disturbed by the activities of the supermarket, will pay little attention. Of course, if the supermarket wished to extend its opening hours, this might lead to the creation of a residents' pressure group, moving them to quadrant B.

During the global financial crisis of 2008 and 2009, there was concern that the largely passive institutional shareholders failed to pay much attention to some of the global banks. It is increasingly argued that a primary role of non-executive directors is to involve and represent these major stakeholders more closely within the business. (**Non-executive directors** sit on the main boards of companies but are charged with providing internal oversight and monitoring of the behaviour of executive directors and senior management of the company. Unlike the executive directors of companies, non-executive directors are not employed as staff by the companies they oversee.) Evidently these stakeholders have an important role to play and should be encouraged to participate more as a means of moderating any tendency by management towards behaviour which is sub-optimal in terms of the objectives of the organisation.

Institutional shareholders include, for example, pension funds or other institutions which may own a relatively high proportion of shares in a company. In the past, such shareholders have tended to play a passive role in the running of the companies in which they invest.

If you have studied B291 Unit 6 (Session 2), you will be familiar with the role of non-executive directors.

2.3 Sources of stakeholder power

The stakeholder matrix shown in Figure 7 can be built on to develop an understanding of whence stakeholders derive power.

Internal stakeholders gain power from:

- *formal authority* awarded to their position or status
- *leadership* (as discussed in Section 1.2.1 onwards, although this may not be formally awarded)
- *control of resources*, human or physical
- *knowledge* – this is the group who knows how to do something.

External stakeholders gain power from:

- *control of strategic resources*, for example, union influence on labour, banks on financial resources
- *involvement* in strategic decisions where an organisation needs their involvement to fulfil a strategy (for example, a farmer granting access to a new development)
- *knowledge*, being external providers of skills such as consultants or sub-contractors
- *influencing* internal stakeholders
- *influencing* powerful external stakeholders.

Activity 2.4 ....

As an OU student, in which quadrant of the Johnson, Scholes and Whittington matrix do you see yourself as a stakeholder with The Open University?

Allow five minutes for this activity.

Feedback   ....

Stakeholders are found in connection with all organisations, not just commercial ones. You might see yourself as having a lot of interest but limited power, falling into quadrant B. However, The Open University will see you as a customer and so as important to the achievement of its objectives. Because of this, The Open University takes great care to contact you, to keep you informed and to ask your opinions on the quality of tuition.

Summary

The term 'stakeholders' is a wide one encompassing any person or group that can influence an organisation. It is no longer appropriate for an organisation to focus solely on its owners in order to maximise the achievement of objectives. An organisation must also satisfy other stakeholders.

Partly because it is such a wide group, individual stakeholders often have different objectives from each other. Identifying these groups and their objectives is a key task of an organisation's management. By mapping their power and influence, an organisation can prioritise the management of any disparate aims. Additionally, the level of interest of stakeholders can change.

SESSION **3 Organisational culture**

Introduction

Upon completion of Session 3 you are expected to be able to:

- explain the 'informal organisation' and its relationship to the formal organisation
- describe the impact of the informal organisation on the business
- define organisational culture
- describe the factors that shape the culture of an organisation
- explain the contribution made by two important writers on culture: Schein and Handy.

Unit 1 explored the concept of formal organisational structures. You saw how people design an organisation which can be a 'centralised' organisation or a 'decentralised' organisation. It may have a 'functional' structure or it may even have a 'matrix' structure. It was established that, whatever structure applies, there should be a clear line of management responsibility so that employees know what they should be doing, and who can require them to do it. Authority in such structures is derived from an individual's position in the formal structure.

This session starts by exploring another form of organisational structure. Within most organisations there exists a parallel structure that is much more subtle than the formal organisational structure, one that is difficult or even impossible to map, not least because it changes as new members join the organisation, or as the task at hand changes. This **informal structure** evolves over time, and power and authority are not derived from an individual's position, but rather from his/her personal skills. Perhaps it is his/her persuasiveness, charisma, knowledge of the organisation or knowledge of an 'issue' that someone else wants resolved. If you consider an organisation with which you are familiar, you will know that informal linkages exist, and that these informal linkages provide powerful avenues of communication and cooperative working. These are explored in more depth later.

Linked to the informal structure, but distinct from it, is the **culture** of an organisation. Terms such as 'culture' can be difficult to explain and understand. This is dealt with in more detail later. For the moment you could think of an organisation's culture in the following way. Imagine that it is your first day in a new job. As part of the process of being inducted into the organisation, you are shown around the different departments and 'the way we do things round here' is explained to you.

Think back to when you first joined an organisation – when you visited it for the first time, when you came out of your first meeting or went home at the end of your first day. There were perhaps things that struck you about the 'feel' of the organisation. You may have noticed the way the place was decorated, the way people dressed, or the way they explained things to you. Even before you understood the organisation's structure, got to know your colleagues, or even found your way around the building, you would have sensed something about the culture of the organisation. Culture has a substantial impact on what happens in an organisation.

3.1 What is an informal organisation?

The formal organisation structure sets rules and procedures that facilitate the alignment of the workforce to the objectives of the organisation. However, most analysts of organisational dynamics accept that these formal procedures cannot cover all circumstances.

A traditional tool of labour unions prosecuting an industrial dispute is to 'work to rule,' meaning that the workforce follows the rules and procedures precisely. This leads to lower productivity resulting from the lack of flexibility of the workforce to overcome problems and bottlenecks in the production process. Working outside of the rules to improve efficiency requires informal consent between the workforce and management.

The workers enforcing a work to rule may not be operating under any union directive but instead through a collective decision not to cooperate with the 'informal consent' that they usually enjoy with the management. So both normal, efficient cooperation and working to rule are examples of the informal organisation functioning. This can be both beneficial and detrimental to the organisation.

If it is accepted that the informal organisation not only exists, but is also a very powerful force, then how should it be defined and, importantly, managed?

The informal organisation could be defined as 'a network of personal and social relationships (alliances, cliques, friendships) that arise as people associate with other people in a work environment' (BusinessDictionary). This is explored in more detail below.

- The make-up of the group will change as people retire or join the organisation. The group will also change depending on particular interests. Some people may be more interested in certain issues than in others.

- People meet in the office or on the shop floor. They talk and share knowledge about the issues that interest them. Information will often pass through this network faster than through formal communication channels, but it may not always be accurate information.

Group norms are discussed in Session 5.
- Additionally, group norms act as a powerful way of ensuring coordinated action by the whole group. Briefly, group norms are shared beliefs about how the group should behave. So, for example, if an informal work to rule takes place, it is the group norm that any individual does not operate outside of the rules. Any breach of group norms will result in the group punishing the individual (perhaps by not talking to them or withdrawing cooperation on another matter).

- Informal leaders are a key part of any group formation. It may be that more than one emerges but however this is structured (informally, of course), the leader(s) can encourage group convergence on common objectives by exercising charisma, persuasion and other personal attributes.

3.1.1   Advantages and disadvantages of the informal organisation

Activity 3.1   ....

What advantages and disadvantages of the informal organisation can you list? Try to do this without looking at our thoughts below.

Spend about ten minutes on this activity.

Feedback   ....

Here are some thoughts.

Advantages	
Commitment	Employees feel that they belong and they may find the job more satisfying.
Information	The informal networks are highly efficient at passing on information. Knowledge about how to complete certain tasks may also be shared. These networks act as an important source of advice for employees and are often the most trusted source of information.
Efficiency	Workers are comfortable working outside formal rules but within the informal organisation's rules. This can enhance flexibility and speed of execution.
Responsiveness	The quality and depth of the informal communication means that individuals are less likely to be surprised by change or by requirements to complete new tasks. Their response will therefore be less bureaucratic (a 'Let's get on with the job and sort out the paperwork later' attitude).
Team working	The informal networks strengthen coordination and reduce reluctance to work across divisions or functions. You are more likely to be working with people you already know, or who are known by a friend. The teams form more quickly with less caution and greater willingness to 'make it work'.

Disadvantages	
Diverging goals	The informal organisation may have goals that conflict with those of the formal organisation.
Misinformation	The information passed on cannot always be relied upon to be accurate. It may contain political agendas or may simply be wrong. Information about negative events will travel quickly and will not be accompanied with any balancing argument. For example, news of redundancies may not be balanced with a statement that there will be no compulsory redundancies. The resultant damage to morale can be considerable.
Exclusion	Individuals may be excluded from informal grouping for non-work related issues. This can damage motivation and result in higher staff turnover.
Quality control	Shortcuts approved by the informal organisation may not adhere to the organisation's desired quality standards, or legal health and safety practices.

3.1.2   Managing the informal organisation

Managers need to reduce the impact of the disadvantages of the informal organisation while capturing any benefits that it may afford. However, by definition, the informal organisation cannot be formally managed. What can managers do to influence the informal organisation? A list of actions that managers may possibly take is given below.

Develop good formal communication. Minimise the risk of incorrect information or of information not being fully explained to the workforce by ensuring that the formal channels are robust and trusted as a consistent source of good information.

Work with the informal leaders. Identify who the informal leaders are and establish a working relationship with them, particularly on key issues. For example, managers can explain any pending changes to staff within the organisational structure and listen to their views. If their views cannot be accommodated, managers can try to ensure that they appreciate that they are not simply being 'brushed off' by explaining the organisation's viewpoint carefully.

Listen to the informal organisation. Meet individuals informally, perhaps at coffee breaks or in the canteen, talk to them and listen to what they have to say.

Act on sensible ideas generated by the informal organisation. Use ideas that the informal organisation generates, provided that they are appropriate. This will reinforce the belief that management is listening.

It is very difficult to influence the informal organisation. When acting informally, managers need to be patient and consistent in order to develop trust.

3.2   What is organisational culture and why is it important?

In the introduction to this session there was a brief discussion on some ways in which you might have been struck by almost intangible features of an organisation when you first encountered it.

Activity 3.2 ....

(a) If a friend applied for a job in your organisation and asked you what it was really like, write down three or four things that you would say.

(b) Imagine your friend then asked you how it differed from the last organisation for which you worked. Write down three or four differences in people's attitudes to work, or the way they behave at work, between your present organisation and the one you last worked for (or another organisation with which you are familiar if you have never changed jobs).

Allow five minutes for this activity.

Feedback ....

(a) You probably found a number of things to tell your friend about – the people you work with, the politics and the gossip, or perhaps your own manager, for example. You may also have mentioned the pressure your team is under, and perhaps commented that some people seem to get on in the organisation whereas others do not. You might also comment on the social aspects of the job, perhaps making new friends easily or the advantages of the sports and social club.

(b) You may have written about how people behave more or less formally in the two organisations. Perhaps in your last organisation you were Bill and your boss was Jill, but here you are Mr Smith and Ms Jones. Maybe people dress more casually or there is a corporate uniform that staff are expected to wear. Perhaps people work flexible rather than set hours.

The 'feel', or culture, of an organisation is more than the sum of all the individual people who work there. It is more than the organisational structure and more than its objectives. Culture is recognised as a significant factor in the way organisations (and the people who manage and work within them) behave. It is also increasingly claimed to be one of the most important influences on organisational success (and failure).

> Peters and Waterman have written a well known book about culture in so-called 'excellent' companies (see the References section for details).

Organisational culture can also be described as 'what the organisation is really like when no one is looking'. If you ask someone a specific question about his/her organisation's culture you may get a slightly puzzled response that 'it's just the way we do things round here'. It may be a small step from this description to the belief that this is the way all organisations are and, indeed, that this is the only way they can be. Of course, there is no single, uniform organisational culture, and a difference in cultures can cause major difficulties when two companies merge, or when two organisations try to collaborate closely with each other.

Edgar Schein (1985) gives richer insights into the issue, breaking organisational culture down into three areas. He starts by observing that an organisation's culture is the most difficult attribute of an organisation to change, not least because so much of it is hidden from view.

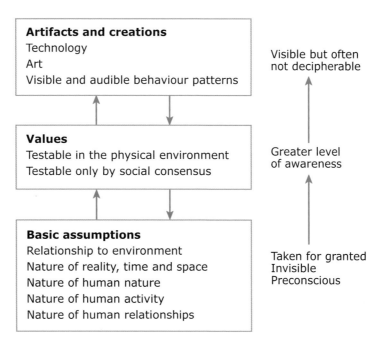

Figure 8 Levels of culture and their interaction
(Source: Schein, 1985, p. 14)

What can be seen from the outside, the 'artifacts and creations' (Schein, 1985, p.14) level as he called it, is easy to ascertain. What can easily be observed are the behaviours of people within the organisation, for example, how they adhere to the norms of behaviour, the rules and customs. There are also the physical manifestations, such as the building, the provision of coffee lounges to facilitate informal communication, the way people dress and the insignia of the organisation. The attitudes of the organisation, namely the formal procedures, can also be recognised.

However, Schein explains that the observable level is built upon the organisation's and its members' values and beliefs. These are harder to observe from outside, although they are likely to be recognised by members of the organisation. It may be that the size of your desk denotes status or that the sales force expects to have preferential parking spaces. It could be that working in a new air-conditioned building is 'the way that an organisation of this stature operates'.

Most difficult to see, often for the individuals themselves, however, is the 'basic assumptions' level. This is usually subconscious and therefore the most difficult level to change. These assumptions inform the values and beliefs and in turn the observable level. An assumption might be that 'working from home is not an effective way of doing things' or 'it is impossible for someone under 30 to have gained sufficient experience to run a department'.

3.2.1   The extent of culture

It is likely that you make various assumptions about how you should behave in any given situation. For example, if you sing in a choir, your working assumption might be that when the conductor asks you to start, you should not question this. This may be based on a belief that, in musical matters, the conductor has the ultimate say, regardless of whether people think that they are right or wrong. Junior members of a choir become aware of this when they first join. This deference to the opinions of a conductor can be considered to be a shared value among choir members.

Activity 3.3

What do you think would be the basic values, ideologies and assumptions of the members of a trade union? How would these manifest themselves?

Allow about five minutes for this activity.

Feedback

It is probable that trade union members would believe that people at work should be protected from arbitrary power exercised by employers and that some collective voice would be required to protect workers. Their beliefs might prompt them actively to encourage new workers to join the trade union. They might also be critical of management and demand high standards of employment relations.

Activity 3.4

What do you think would (or should) be the basic values, ideologies and assumptions of a group of accountants? How would these manifest themselves?

Spend about five minutes thinking about this activity.

Feedback   ....

You probably thought that accountants should behave professionally and impartially in their work. They might therefore be just as (or more) loyal to the accountancy profession as to the particular organisation for which they work. They are likely to support formal, standardised ways of doing things (e.g., accounting standards). One visible manifestation of all this might be widespread wearing of dark grey or black suits!

This question relating to culture reflects two very different views of what culture is.

Is culture something an organisation is or something it has? Are the shared values and assumptions of a choir so deep-rooted that they cannot be changed because they are inherent in the choir, or can the members of the choir be influenced to change their attitudes? Is it possible to distinguish between organisational culture – the values, ideologies and assumptions of the organisation arising from the collective experiences of its members – and corporate culture – the work-specific assumptions that arise, usually from senior management action?

3.2.2   The manifestation of culture

Schein's approach suggests ways in which culture can become apparent. This implies that you can identify aspects of culture from a range of more concrete factors: office decoration and layout are a couple of these. In your own workplace you can probably see that how it is organised reflects the organisation's ethos, which, in turn, influences the way you work. Are there notice boards with lots of edicts from senior management on them? This would suggest that it is somewhat bureaucratic. Are there lots of primary colours, informal seating areas and coffee machines? That could be characteristic of a business that values informality and/or creativity.

Some management writers mention stories that are told within and about the organisation and explain that these act as another manifestation of culture. Does your organisation say that it is committed to breaking the **glass ceiling** and ensuring that women climb up the corporate ladder? If so, are there any female senior managers? Whose successes do the members of staff talk about in the bar? Do those stories reflect the corporate goal of equal opportunities? If not, might there be a cultural problem in achieving that goal?

Dress and rituals are other features of culture that vary from one organisation to another.

Activity 3.5   ....

The Bach Choir and the Hackney Singers are two London choirs that both put on high quality performances. The male members of the Bach Choir wear dinner jackets for their concerts. The choir comes on to the stage in a formal procession. There is no talking on the stage before or after performances and the choir does not applaud its soloists. The Hackney Singers' men, on the other hand, wear open-necked shirts. There is no formal procession on to the stage and the singers talk animatedly to each other before and after concerts and applaud wildly when the orchestra and soloists take their bows.

Can you identify any values, ideologies or assumptions from this?

Allow five minutes for this activity.

Feedback   ....

You would probably assume that the Bach Choir is a rather more staid organisation, whose members believed (perhaps justifiably) that they are musically important. You might think that they value formality and conformity. In contrast, you might consider the Hackney Singers an inclusive organisation that does not expect people to own dinner jackets in order to be able to make music. Their enthusiasm for what they achieve, you might conclude, transcends other considerations.

3.2.3   The importance of culture

You should not underestimate the importance of culture. It has an impact on every aspect of how an organisation works, as the following example illustrates.

> **A culture for equal opportunities**
>
> An organisation with a very explicit commitment to equal opportunities introduced a whole series of family-friendly policies and practices to encourage women to return to work after maternity leave. These included part time and job-share arrangements as well as leave for parents to care for children who were ill or dependent.
>
> While these were supposedly being implemented across the whole organisation, it became apparent that managers and colleagues in different departments were giving very different informal messages to women about their family responsibilities and their decision to return to work. There were many different views about the role that mothers should play. Women lower down the organisation often felt the disapproval of colleagues and managers. These included older women, who felt that they had coped without any of these supportive arrangements, and resented the special treatment they saw being afforded to younger women.
>
> Female managers felt a different sort of pressure. The culture of the organisation was one where breakfast and evening meetings were a frequent occurrence and where a lot of informal business was conducted over a drink at the end of the day. They found this hard to reconcile with the formal family-friendly policies.

The example in the box above illustrates how culture and behaviour can inhibit the implementation of organisational policies or initiatives. When people are asked to do things that conflict with their deeply held values, they are likely to try to find ways to resist.

Activity 3.6   ....

Can you think of any ways in which the informal behaviour of staff inhibits the achievement of your organisation's goals?

Allow five minutes to think about this activity.

Feedback   ....

What you found will be specific to your own organisation. In certain areas there has been concern about behaviour. For example, there has been a good deal of concern about the extent to which police officers have practised Freemasonry in their leisure time, on the grounds that this could result in the development of shared values that might conflict with the official values of the police force. Other value-based organisations might have similar concerns. For example, the Refugee Council would be likely to be concerned if its staff associated themselves in their spare time with organisations seeking repatriation of refugees.

3.3 Models of culture

Unit 1 introduced you to different models of structure (functional, product, matrix, etc.). This section looks at some models of culture.

Charles Handy (1985) identified four types of culture. Handy also named the cultural types after Greek gods.

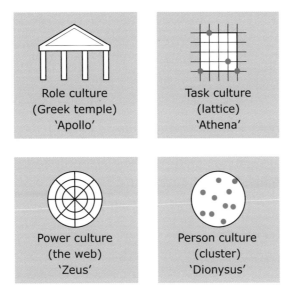

Figure 9 Four cultural models
(Source: adapted from Handy, 1985, *Understanding Organizations*, pp. 181–190)

Role culture

In contrast to the person culture, it is impersonality that is central to a **role culture**. This can be represented as a building (see Figure 9) held together by columns and beams, each of which has a specific role to play in keeping the building standing. The organisation is seen as a set of inter-related roles, with individuals as role occupants. Communications tend to be formalised into systems and procedures, both horizontal and vertical.

This is an organisation that likes straight lines. It is likely to be managed rather than led. Certainty, predictability, continuity and stability are seen as important organisational virtues in a role culture. Processes for training and developing expertise are important, so that the people involved in the organisation can contribute appropriately. Independence and initiative will probably be less highly valued than professionalism and reliability.

Activity 3.7 ....

What kind of structure would you expect in an organisation with a role culture? (Look back at Unit 1 if you need to.)

Allow five minutes for this activity.

Feedback ....

A functional structure is probably the most likely answer, although you would not be wrong if you suggested a product structure.

> **We are all dispensable**
>
> 'You work a 60 hour week for ten years in this role culture. What happens when you are run over by a bus? Sure, your colleagues will grieve a little – or a lot – depending on your popularity. Then someone will go to the filing cabinet, take out your job description and set about finding a replacement.
>
> 'Maybe sometimes we all need reminding that we are replaceable, in any culture! In the person culture it may prove harder: do you have a 'job description'? In the power culture, what happens when the person at the centre of the spider's web is the one who falls under the bus?
>
> 'Maybe we should take up Charles Handy's suggestion that managers in role cultures should try writing their own obituaries as a way of assessing their priorities: do we really want to be remembered for always submitting our monthly report on time?'

In practice, organisations may contain features of all or none of Handy's four categories, but the models can still aid analysis of how an organisation operates. The example in the box shows how the realisation that the company had a role culture made a manager reflect on how it valued its individuals.

Task culture

The dominant feature of **task culture** is its job or project orientation, hence its representation as a net or lattice, in which groups can be assembled in different ways, depending on what needs to be done (see Figure 9). Competent people who enjoy new challenges and are stimulated by joining different teams often prefer a task culture. The notion of work as problem solving will probably be a major feature of a task culture, with people relying on their concerted abilities to deal with new situations rather than applying tried and tested formulae. Coordinators and team leaders, rather than managers, are central figures.

There is an air of youthful self-confidence and energy about task cultures that can be uncomfortable for those who need the security of agreed procedures to shape their work and their relationships. Task cultures are typical of IT companies, particularly those involved in software development.

Activity 3.8 ....

What kind of structure would you expect an organisation with a task culture to have? (Hint: look at Unit 1 again if you need to.)

Allow about five minutes for this activity.

Feedback ....

You might expect to find the organisation to be based on project teams that change their membership depending on what projects the team is working on.

Power culture

A **power (or web) culture** can be pictured as a web (as shown in Figure 9) because the key to the whole organisation sits, spider-like, in the centre, connected to and pulling the strings of an ever-widening network of intimates and influence. The organisation is very much like a web: it exists to enable the decisions of those at the centre to be carried out.

The key to success in a power culture lies in employing 'the right sort of people' and ensuring that new recruits will fit in satisfactorily. Many organisations with a power culture have the feel and ethos of a large extended family and many family companies fall into this category.

Person culture

Power and task cultures assume that it is the organisation's purposes that are of overriding importance. In contrast, a **person culture** puts individuals and their interests first and sees the organisation as a sort of means to an end. It is a resource on which individuals can draw to enhance their own talents, abilities or concerns. The person culture is represented by a group of loosely clustered dots (see Figure 9). In this culture, commitment to the organisation for its own sake is likely to be limited.

Groupings such as an artists' cooperative, an academic 'think-tank' or a consulting partnership typify this sort of culture, where people are driven primarily by their own personal and professional values.

Activity 3.9 ....

Using Handy's classification, how would you describe the culture of your organisation or one with which you are familiar?

Which attributes would you suggest managers should have in order to be well suited to that culture? Identify someone successful in your chosen organisation. How has that person 'got ahead'?

Spend about ten minutes working on this activity.

Feedback ....

You may have found that Handy's approach offers insights into your understanding of culture. However, there is a danger that Handy's four cultures are taken as fixed or given styles. An organisation may be seen as developing a particular prevailing ethos that managers are responsible for identifying and maintaining: 'if you work here, this is how we do things; this is our culture'. Culture tends to be seen as something an organisation has, rather than something that is created by everyone involved in the organisation and which may evolve over time. There is little recognition that cultures are often about conflict as well as agreement, or that they can include some people but exclude others.

3.4 Factors that shape the culture of an organisation

How does a culture within an organisation evolve? Clearly with a small organisation the culture of the organisation is likely to be strongly influenced by the founder, who is, possibly, also the owner. However, the founder also has a major influence on the culture of a larger organisation. Looking back to Schein's three determinants of culture it is not hard to visualise a strong founder having a lasting influence on the assumptions (level 3) and the values and beliefs (level 2). Once these assumptions and values are formed, they become embedded in the minds of employees. They become part of the culture and are hard to change even when the founder leaves.

History also plays an important role in shaping culture. A software company formed in 2010 is likely to have a much looser culture than a manufacturing company formed a hundred years earlier. However, it is not just the era in which a company was formed that influences the culture today. Also important are all of the events and the stories that influence the individual employees. For example, a 'larger than life' leader who first won contracts overseas may be remembered and talked about years after he has left, and his style of doing business may leave a permanent mark on the organisation's culture. It becomes an assumption that his way is an effective way of doing things.

Of course, leadership has an important role to play in forming culture. A charismatic and strong leader is likely to select senior managers who conform to his or her style. In turn, this influences the organisational culture. Note that we say 'influence' rather than using a stronger term, given that it is difficult to change the underlying assumptions of employees. Even a strong leader may have difficulty doing much more than influencing culture.

An organisation in France is likely to have a different culture from an organisation in America or one in China. National and regional values also influence culture.

Handy's cultures can be linked to the type of influence that might have been dominant in their formation.

Power culture. This is likely to have a strong influence from one individual, the person at the centre of the web.

Role culture. A bureaucratic culture that is influenced by rules and procedures.

Task culture. This is shaped by the needs of the task and the culture focuses on results.

Person culture. This cultural type is heavily influenced by the collective aspirations of individuals.

3.4.1   Negotiated cultures and subcultures

Another way of thinking about culture is to look at the different values that people themselves bring to their organisation. Through their inputs, people construct a sense of organisational identity. This means that there may be more than one culture in an organisation (or part of it). In reality there will always be a variety of cultures and **subcultures** to which different groups subscribe. Different groups in an organisation develop their own distinctive ways of interpreting and explaining what is happening. An example of how a range of cultures can exist within an organisation is illustrated in the box below.

> **Subcultures**
>
> The company was a household name, and was widely regarded as a model employer. It promoted itself as being socially responsible and having a caring attitude towards its staff. It had a strong role culture, and outsiders often referred to its employees as 'clones'. However, the reality was somewhat different.
>
> • The production department was located on a separate site. Its staff prided themselves on being different: they had their own management

restaurant, worked different hours, and no one wore suits. There were few female employees, and no women in management. They had a strong local identity, an active recreation club, and their works' football team competed successfully in the local league. Other people on the site felt that the production staff had more in common with their suppliers than with other parts of the company. Few production staff had experience of other parts of the company.

- Marketing staff considered themselves somewhat superior to the rest of the company. Their average age was lower, most of them were graduates, and they all travelled a great deal in their work. They tended to eat and drink off-site, many lived a considerable distance away, and everyone took care how they dressed. Women made up more than half the staff, although they were still in the minority at the management level. Few marketing staff expected to stay in their present jobs or on the same site for long.

- Research and development staff were located on the main company site, but they mixed little with their commercial or administrative colleagues. They consisted of two distinct groups: the laboratory technicians, who were predominantly female and mostly unqualified, with a high staff turnover and little opportunity for career progression; and the scientists, who included men and women, but had no female senior managers. Many of the scientists had been with the company all their working lives, and their interests and contacts were dominated by their professional specialism. They belonged to strong networks of scientists working in different companies, and saw the opportunity to attend conferences as compensation for the repetitive and banal work in which they were engaged for most of the time.

All three groups probably had a higher loyalty to their own subculture than to the company, which ensured that any change initiative never achieved more than partial success.

3.5 Changing culture

You may be interested to know that many books have been written about managing culture.

It is usually the job of senior management to ensure that an appropriate culture is found in a particular organisation.

In the early 1980s, Tom Peters and Bob Waterman, partners in the management consultancy firm, McKinsey and Company, explored what made for 'excellence' in large commercial companies in the USA. They concluded that success was based on a strong corporate culture, on core values of customer service, innovation and quality, and on managers who encouraged initiative and facilitated a culture where people actually wanted to work and to succeed. Organisations that had this kind of culture performed best.

The work of Peters and Waterman (1982) has been criticised by some observers, and some of the firms they described as excellent have subsequently hit hard times. However, it was the spur for managers in all sorts of organisations to embark on cultural change programmes to try to become excellent. Managers believed that if they could change their organisation's culture, its performance could be significantly improved.

Activity 3.10   ....

You have learned enough about culture during this session to make it likely that you are asking yourself: 'Why on earth did people think that changing culture was an easy route to excellence? How can people think that they can change people's deeply held values?' You can now clearly see that any organisational change based on adapting cultures is very challenging. Why might managers want to change cultures? What actions would help them at least to start to mould an organisational culture?

Allow five minutes for this activity.

Feedback

Some people think that the sheer arrogance of the idea was breathtaking.

The short answer is that changing people's values seemed easier than managing. If managers could get people to think the same way as themselves, they could dispense with rules, procedures and sanctions and just watch people getting on with their work.

However, this does not mean that managers cannot influence an organisation's culture, for example, by promoting a more business-like view or introducing the idea that long-term investment is more important than 'profits today'. At worst, they can sack everyone and replace them with people who fit with management's views of what the organisation's values should be. At best, management can recognise that organisational culture – what the organisation is – can only be influenced on a long-term basis, but that corporate culture – what the organisation has – might be influenced more readily.

Managers need to understand and respect the cultures of their organisation as the accumulated products of the lives and experiences of their staff. At the same time, if they want to make changes, they should be prepared to encounter cultural conflicts. Change programmes therefore have to be managed in such a way that staff members are aware of the reasons why change is required and are helped to adjust to it.

'I've been restructured.'

Summary

This session has discussed the informal organisation and explained what culture is and why it is important. You have been given some models describing cultures and you have seen the importance of occupational cultures. The session expressed healthy scepticism about culture change programmes, but recognised that major change is likely to result in cultural resistance that managers have to address in some way.

You should now be in a better position to understand the culture of your organisation and to appreciate how it affects your own behaviour. You should also be aware of the difficulties inherent in seeking to change an organisation's culture.

SESSION **4 Motivation and reward systems within the organisation**

Introduction

Upon completion of Session 4 you are expected to be able to:

- discuss motivation and explain its importance to the organisation, teams and individuals
- explain content and process theories of motivation, including the theories of Maslow, Herzberg, McGregor and Vroom
- discuss and identify types of intrinsic and extrinsic reward
- explain how reward systems can be designed and implemented to motivate teams and individuals.

Session 1 looked at management and leadership and explored how leaders encourage their followers to aim for a common objective. A major component of that is motivation. In this session, you are going to look at what makes people work and what makes them work harder. The idea of motivation is central to the understanding of behaviour and performance at work and, over the years, there have been many theories about motivation that are relevant to management. Two theories will be considered in detail: one which seeks to explain how people's needs affect their motivation to work, and one which looks at motivation in terms of the link between effort expended and the expectation of an associated reward.

4.1 Human needs as motivators

A core concept underpinning motivation theory is that people have a need they want to fulfil. That need is not always the same for all people or, indeed, for the same person at different times.

Abraham Maslow's (1943) **theory of motivation** emerged from his work in the USA during the 1940s and asserts that the best way to motivate someone is to understand what his/her next need is.

He believed that everyone needs to provide for his/her own and their family's basic survival, that is, to provide food, shelter and clothing. He considered these basic requirements to be a person's practical and biological needs which might be achieved on a modest wage, from, perhaps, a part time job or temporary work. These are shown in Figure 10. When someone is striving to fulfil these basic needs, these needs are very important to them. However, once someone has attained sufficient wealth to cover the basic needs (which are commonly referred to as 'physiological needs'– see Figure 10), their importance to the individual reduces. Instead, individuals focus on keeping the basics they have achieved. They are looking for their 'safety needs': job security, the provision of a good pension and good working conditions. People may even trade a small amount of income in exchange for more certainty about their future employment.

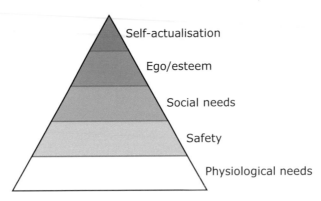

Figure 10   Maslow's hierarchy of needs
(Source: derived from Maslow, 1943, *passim*)

Maslow's **hierarchy of needs** has been a very important framework in management theory.

Continuing up Maslow's hierarchy, people who have satisfied their safety needs with a safety net will aspire to 'social needs', by building a network of friends, colleagues and family in order to develop a social life. This might be fulfilled in the workplace by the provision of a social club, or even something as simple as coffee break-out areas. After this stage, the focus of individuals starts to change. They want to improve their status: they have an 'ego or esteem need'. They want to be respected so that they may prefer a promotion to a pay rise, particularly if that promotion represents another step on the ladder that they aim to climb.

The pinnacle of Maslow's hierarchy is **self-actualisation**. He believed that we all strive for this, for a feeling that we have succeeded, to feel that life is worthwhile and that we have done, or are doing, all that can be expected of us. Maslow considered that this is rarely achieved, but if it is, we have 'arrived'.

This idea of a hierarchy of needs is now regarded as being a little simplistic. Not only can individuals be motivated by more than one need at a time, but sometimes the needs may conflict. Furthermore, regional cultural differences may alter the hierarchy: Europeans, for example, place more emphasis on their work/life balance than do Americans. Nevertheless, the notion of human needs as motivators contains some important ideas.

Frederick Herzberg (1959) proposed a similar **duality theory** of motivators and hygiene factors. He argued that there are certain factors that are essential to achieving job satisfaction, which he called **hygiene factors**. The absence of any hygiene factor would weaken efforts to motivate and would have a **dis-satisfier effect**.

Table 1   Herzberg's hygiene factors

Hygiene or dis-satisfier factors	Motivational or satisfier factors
Working conditions	Recognition
Staff relations	Personal growth
Company rules and administration	Achievement
Basic pay	Responsibility

(Source: adapted from Hertzberg, 1959, as cited in Herzberg et al., 2005)

Take a few minutes to map Herzberg's hygiene and motivational factors to Maslow's hierarchy of needs. You will see just how similar they are. The hygiene factors map to the physiological needs and safety net while motivational factors correlate strongly to social needs, ego and self-fulfilment.

Activity 4.1 ....

Consider your own feelings when you decided to study B292. Perhaps you had recently started work or had left full time education and wanted to prepare for work. What drove you to choose to devote so much time and energy to your studies? Use the theories of both Maslow and Herzberg to explain your decision.

Spend ten minutes on this activity.

Feedback ....

Only you can comment on your motivational forces, but if you are studying while working full time the motivation must be strong. Perhaps you feel that you have obtained your physiological needs but wish to secure a longer-term career, or the ability to switch employers should you desire to do so. Looking at Herzberg's motivational factors, you may be motivated towards personal growth and recognition as a means to fulfil your safety needs (per Maslow).

4.2 The inclination of individuals to be led or managed

Another school of thought concerning leadership and motivation centres on the attitude of the individual. Are individuals naturally inclined to work or must they be coerced?

The differences between these competing theories of human behaviour at work were neatly summarised by Douglas McGregor in his book, *The Human Side of Enterprise* (1960) as **Theory X** and **Theory Y**. They are summarised in Table 2.

Table 2   Theory X and Theory Y

Theory X	Theory Y
The average human being dislikes work and will avoid it if possible.	The expenditure of physical and mental effort is as natural as play or rest. The ordinary person does not inherently dislike work. According to the conditions, it may be a source of satisfaction or punishment.
Because of this human characteristic of dislike of work, most people must be coerced, controlled, directed or threatened with punishment to get them to put in adequate effort towards the achievement of organisational objectives.	External control is not the only means for obtaining effort. People will exercise self-direction and self-control in the service of objectives to which they are committed.
The average human being prefers to be directed, wishes to avoid responsibility, has very little ambition, and wants security above all.	The average human being learns, under proper conditions, not only to accept, but to seek, responsibility.

You saw both these theories of management in Session 1.

According to McGregor, Theory X is based on the traditional managerial approach of direction and control (Taylorism), while Theory Y fits in better with Mayo's approaches.

'Well of course you outperformed me. The incentives were stacked in your favour.'

Activity 4.2

Think about an organisation in which you have been involved or one that you know well. Try to identify one manager whom you could describe as a Theory X manager and another whom you could identify as a Theory Y manager. In the column headed 'Particular behaviour' in the tables below, describe the behaviour of the manager that matches the summary of his/her beliefs in the left-hand column. In the column headed 'Consequences', summarise what you think were the consequences of that behaviour.

What conclusions can you draw from this analysis?

Spend about thirty minutes on this activity.

Theory X manager

Theory X beliefs	Particular behaviour	Consequences
People have an inherent dislike of work.		
People must be coerced, controlled, directed or threatened.		
People wish to be directed rather than accept responsibility.		

Theory Y manager

Theory Y beliefs	Particular behaviour	Consequences
People do not dislike work: it can be a source of satisfaction.		
People will exercise self-direction and self-control to achieve objectives to which they are committed.		
People learn to accept and to seek responsibility.		

Feedback ....

When you ask people to describe the best manager for whom they have ever worked, it is likely that they will mention that person's values. For example, they may say that they believed that the manager was concerned for them as individuals and wanted to see them develop and achieve things. This suggests that most people appreciate Theory Y behaviour in a manager, whatever their own beliefs about human behaviour. However, there is no one best way to manage. For example, you would probably be unimpressed by a manager who spent an afternoon discussing your development needs if the consequences of this were that the firm did not have the funds to pay for the necessary training – or even to pay your salary.

4.3 Expectancy theory: performance and reward as motivators

A third dimension of motivational theory is based upon the assumption that if an individual values a reward, and believes that it is attainable, then he/she will be encouraged to put in more effort to achieve it.

Let us assume that your partner, or a friend, has promised to reward you with something you value if you attain a distinction in B292 – perhaps a well earned holiday in the Caribbean. If your TMA results are good but only just at the level needed to obtain a distinction, you might feel you needed to put in a considerable effort to push your examination marks up to a level where an overall distinction is achievable. You would like the reward but might doubt that you could achieve it. In this situation, you would be probably put in enough work to pass, but not the extra work to get a distinction.

If on the other hand your TMA marks are all well above the minimum needed to get a distinction and you are reasonably confident that you could also gain a distinction in the examination, you are more likely to put in the extra effort to ensure an overall distinction.

4.3.1 Expectancy theory

This logical concept (**expectancy theory**) was first developed by Victor Vroom in the 1960s (Vroom, 1964). It is an extremely useful and important theory, so it is worth looking at in some detail. Vroom's basic model considered that three factors influence the effort an individual will apply to a task, as set out below.

Valence. The value that an individual places on the reward.

Expectancy. The level of confidence an individual has in his/her ability to complete the task.

Instrumentality. The level of belief he/she has that if the task is achieved, he/she will get the reward.

Vroom attempted to place numerical values between 0 and 1 on each dimension. For example, the valence might be worth 0.5 to an individual if he or she places a moderate value on the reward. The end result was an equation where:

$$\text{effort} = \text{valence} \times \text{probability of expectancy} \times \text{probability of instrumentality}$$

One of the main problems with the theory is that the reward is not provided for effort, but for performance. Lyman Porter and Edward Lawler (1968) added some useful enhancements to Vroom's model describing the linkage between effort and performance. They argued that performance is a factor of the following.

Effort. This is as depicted in Vroom's formula.

Skills and ability. It can be demotivating to be given a task and then to realise that it is quite beyond your skills and abilities. It is a manager's responsibility to ensure that the person in question is capable of doing the job or that he/she will be able to do it once he/she has received training or development.

Role. Individuals will perceive the role based on the description provided. Clear objectives are therefore a key factor.

Resources. This is linked to individuals' perception of the role. They will be demotivated if they perceive a lack of resources. Resources include having sufficient time to complete the task, and having too many tasks to complete in too little time is highly demotivating.

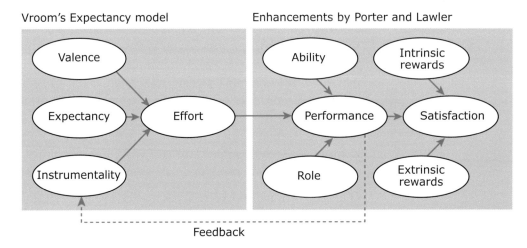

Figure 11 Vroom's expectancy model with enhancements by Porter and Lawler (Source: adapted from Porter and Lawler, 1968, p. 165)

Intrinsic rewards tend to arise from performance of the work itself and so are psychological rather than money-based. Such rewards therefore relate to job satisfaction.

Extrinsic rewards differ from intrinsic rewards in that they are dependent on decisions made by other people. Examples of extrinsic rewards include pay and other work-related benefits.

Vroom's model can be explained using the analogy of wanting a distinction in B292. You have decided to expend the effort but the outcome is not just about the effort that you need to put in: you must be capable of obtaining a distinction. In other words, you must understand the subject well and have experience at passing examinations which, combined with the effort, should produce the desired outcome. The other dimension is your perception of the role you will need to perform. You will need sufficient time for study, probably in a quiet room away from any distractions.

The linkage between effort and performance is one of the weaknesses in Vroom's original model of expectancy. The other problem many people have with the model is the apparent mathematical precision. Each of Vroom's original inputs is only an *estimate* of what the individual perceives. You may feel that the inter-relationship between the factors is informative, but that to place any mathematical certainty on this is questionable. After all, the ratio between expectancy, instrumentality and valence will vary according to an individual's perception.

4.3.2 The link between effort and performance

It is very important for anyone interested in improving motivation to understand the link between effort and performance. As you work through the next activity you will see why it is up to the manager to ensure that this link is strong.

Activity 4.3

Imagine a small software producer providing 'apps' (applications) for mobile phones. The firm needs to expand its market research team to discover fresh ideas for apps. Recruits will only receive basic pay but will receive a generous bonus based on the sales of apps that were developed from their research.

Jane has just finished her design degree and has been recruited. Jane was a mature student and is a single mother aged 31. She is delighted to have the job as it enables her to move out of her parents' home into an apartment near the centre of town.

Today is her first day at work and she is shown to her desk and told to start work. She knows she needs to come up with fresh ideas but has no idea where to start work.

(a) At what stage is Jane on Maslow's hierarchy of needs?

(b) Has Jane been given the basic hygiene factors as described by Hertzberg?

(c) Try to apply Vroom's expectancy theory to Jane's situation.

Allow ten minutes for this activity.

Feedback

(a) You might feel that as a single mother Jane's physiological needs have been met: she has a job but is likely to struggle financially unless she can enhance her income through the bonus scheme. She is likely to be looking for more certainty about her income levels and some additional work-related benefits such as a good pension scheme. She is therefore still likely to be striving to achieve the full safety net that she desires.

(b) It is likely that Jane has a sense of achievement in getting the job but the other Hertzberg motivators are likely to come only when she gains more experience. The basic pay level is, however, likely to remain a hygiene or dis-satisfier factor for the time being: she will not be motivated while she is on only the basic pay.

(c) Vroom's expectancy theory is interesting in that it helps to explain the importance of the bonus scheme. The scheme is clear and Jane can be confident that if she helps to develop more apps, she will be rewarded (it has high instrumentality). Similarly, the bonus is important to her (it has high valence). The only question is Jane's ability to achieve the target (expectancy). Jane will gain confidence in this as she settles into the job and then will be strongly motivated to perform. She will see a clear link between her effort and the reward.

4.3.3 The link between performance and outcome (satisfaction)

In a work situation, you need feedback to tell you how well you are performing. If you are selling products then volume of sales is one important piece of information. However, what about the quality of the relationships you have with your clients?

Where objective measures are quantifiable, such as the number of sales per month, feedback is fairly straightforward, but other important aspects of performance are not so easy to measure. In some jobs, feedback is often lacking, partly for this reason. From what is known about expectancy theory, it is clear that if a person is unsure about how he/she is performing, then the link between performance and satisfaction, or outcome, is likely to be weak. Remember that it matters less whether the link is actually there than the individual's belief that it is there.

Activity 4.4

Can you think how an organisation might introduce an obvious link between performance and rewards?

Allow about five minutes for this activity.

Feedback

If an organisation introduced a performance-related pay scheme this would indicate to its employees that there was a strong link between performance and reward. Whether a performance-related pay scheme is, in fact, a good motivator is another matter, as you will see.

It is clear from studying Maslow's theory that people are not only motivated by the prospect of more pay or promotion (extrinsic rewards). Intrinsic rewards, such as the satisfaction of a job done well, the feeling of having learned a new skill or of contributing to a worthwhile project, act as rewards in themselves for some people. There is a role for the manager here in strengthening the link between performance and satisfaction by ensuring that people receive both feedback and specific praise for their individual contributions.

Activity 4.5

Before moving on, you should try to relate these ideas to your own experience by answering the questions below. You may like to do this on a separate piece of paper as you should find the activity useful in thinking about your own career and work aspirations. The following three questions relate to Maslow's theory.

1   Which of Maslow's needs are important to you at the moment?
2   Which of them are you able to satisfy in your present or most recent job?
3   How else might you seek to satisfy these needs?

Spend about ten minutes on this activity.

Feedback

Your response to these questions will be very personal, but they should have made you think about why you work and what motivates you personally to perform well. It might be useful to review this activity from time to time to see if your responses to the questions change.

There have been many studies of motivation over the years, and you would be right to think that understanding what motivates individuals is a very complex business. Schein (1970) thought that the best way to tackle the problem was to think about it in terms of the psychological contract that exists between an employer and the employee.

The last section of this session examines this concept briefly. It will help you to understand more about what influences a person's behaviour at work.

4.4 The psychological contract

When people join an organisation, they usually enter into a formal contract of employment with their employer. This states, among other things, the work that is required in return for financial consideration, the amount of holiday entitlement and various other benefits. However, Schein observed that, in addition to this formal contract, there is also an **unwritten** or **psychological contract**, which, in reality, amounts to a series of expectations on both sides. These expectations relate to the way in which employees expect the organisation to treat them and the way in which the organisation expects employees to behave in return. So, for example, an individual could reasonably expect that he/she would not suddenly be downgraded to a lesser job. A company could reasonably expect that an employee would not share company secrets with a competitor.

Expectations of employer and employee form an unwritten psychological contract.

Although the psychological contract is not written down or made explicit, it works because both sides accept the notion of authority. A company has the authority to tell the people who work for it what to do in the interests of the company's overall strategy. The employee, in deciding to join a company, implicitly consents to submit to this authority, even at times when it might be against his/her inclinations. This does not mean that the company can take advantage of people or exert force over them. The authority has to be seen as legitimate or people will withdraw their cooperation and consent. For example, there has to be a proper system for appointing or promoting people which is seen to be fair.

From what has been said so far, you may think that the contract is weighted in favour of the organisation. What, then, is the value of the contract for the employee? In many organisations today the move is towards giving people more 'say' in the way they carry out their work. This means that individuals feel that they can influence what happens in the organisation, or at least ensure that they are not exploited. This is the other side of the psychological contract.

There are three important implications of the psychological contract that you should think about.

1 Most people belong to more than one organisation or group and they will therefore have more than one psychological contract. Few people try to satisfy all of their needs through work.

2 The problem with a psychological contract is that it may not be viewed in the same way by both sides and this can lead to problems. For example, an individual might feel exploited by his/her organisation while, on the other hand, his/her manager may believe that this person is lazy or uncooperative. The root of the problem may be that they each have a different interpretation of what constitutes the psychological contract between them.

3 People, as well as organisations, change over time and the psychological contract will change too. As organisations become increasingly complex, more is demanded of their employees in terms of, for example, their ability to handle technology or their capacity to think creatively. As companies become more and more

dependent upon their human resources, they have to examine their assumptions about them and adjust the psychological contract accordingly.

Understanding what motivates people when they are at work can help the manager who wants to find ways of improving individual performance. However, even if you are not a manager, recognising that different people are motivated differently can be useful in trying to understand human behaviour.

Summary

In this session you have seen that individuals undoubtedly have different motivational needs which affect their approach to work. It can be helpful to understand the basis upon which individuals will exert effort.

These are important considerations for anyone who is responsible for the performance of others. You should also have discovered that understanding your own personal motivation can be useful in thinking about your own career.

As well as the formal written agreement between an employee and an employer, both sides also hold certain unwritten expectations, which form a psychological contract between them. It is important to try to understand what unwritten expectations an individual holds, as these can also be a key to behaviour.

At the start of this unit you were reminded that organisational life is changing and so too is the nature of the relationship between the employer and the employee. A job for life – something that used to be implied, especially when an individual joined a large organisation – can no longer be guaranteed nor, in many cases, is it even what the employee wants. This is reflected in the psychological contract. Individuals are not necessarily trained and developed for a career within a particular company any longer. They are, however, provided with opportunities to keep their skills updated to protect their career prospects, whether these are inside or outside that particular company.

This session, through exploring motivation and human behaviour at work, has begun to consider the manager's role in terms of human resource management. This will be continued in Session 5 which looks at teams and groups.

SESSION 5 Groups and group effectiveness

Introduction

Upon completion of Session 5 you are expected to be able to:

- describe the main characteristics of individual and group behaviour
- outline the contributions of individuals and teams to organisational success
- explain the differences between a group and a team
- define the purpose of a team
- list the characteristics of effective and ineffective teams
- describe the methods that can be used to build the team and improve team effectiveness.

In the previous session you looked at what motivates individuals to perform well. However, in most organisations people do not work in isolation but in groups of some kind, whether they are committees or project teams, where outcomes depend upon the contribution of each individual to a task. In such cases it can be easier to evaluate the performance of the group as a whole rather than that of each individual. Group working can provide some of the elements which, in themselves, act as motivators for individuals, such as offering work that is seen to be meaningful and adds value, the fulfilment of personal social needs and opportunities to learn from others and to receive feedback.

Potentially, a group should be able to achieve more than an individual working on his/her own, but it will only do so once its members have begun to regard themselves as a group, having shared aims and norms. The needs of the group demand a certain degree of conformity from its members. This may mean that individual behaviour changes as a result of group pressure to conform. Furthermore, formal work groups need to be carefully constructed to maximise the potential benefit. If a group is constructed inappropriately, the whole may not be better than the sum of its individual parts.

All of this has important implications for you, whether as a manager or as a member of a group and so, for the whole of this session, you will be examining ideas associated with groups and group performance. The session starts by defining what a group is and then goes on to take a look at group working and group effectiveness and finally goes on to draw some conclusions about the management of groups and teams.

5.1 What is a group?

If you were asked to define a group, you might begin by saying that it consists of more than one person and that these people meet together from time to time. This is a good start, but this definition could equally apply to a random collection of people, who wait at a bus stop each day. Could they really be termed a group? How would you regard people who do not actually meet but for most of the time communicate electronically?

Handy (1985) describes a group of individuals as 'any collection of people who perceive themselves to be a group' (pp. 150–51).

Charles Handy has contributed much to the understanding of groups and group behaviour.

You should note in particular that it is the *individuals* who define themselves as a group. What Handy means by this is that managers can only encourage or facilitate the formation of formal groups. For example, they may establish committees, but the individuals must feel part of the group for the group to work well.

Conversely, individuals may form groups without management encouragement. These would be informal groups which might be the people who work in the post room of a large office complex or the people who interact with each other when shipments of goods are delivered: the driver, the warehouse manager and so on.

Handy went on to explain that groups have the following characteristics, as set out below.

A clear sense of identity. They are clear about who is in the group and who is not.

Common goals. They have goals, such as maximising sales, negotiating for higher pay or more holiday, etc.

Group norms. These define the group's way of behaving. This is usually an informal understanding, although occasionally it is enshrined in formal rules. If it is informal, it is no weaker, and may be stronger than if enshrined in a formal set of rules.

As an example of this, assume that you form a study group with fellow B292 students. You would not permit a student of another subject to join your group. You know who should be a member and who should not be. Perhaps you agree that it is a local group so that you can meet and discuss the module. If you are based in Colchester, you would not expect someone in Birmingham to join your group.

Your goals are clear: to help each other to understand the topics and prepare for TMAs and the examination. You agree to meet at a local public house. You do not expect people to be late and you have developed a rule that you have a shared pot to fund any refreshments. You have an accepted agenda whereby you spend about thirty minutes in informal chat before getting down to the task.

★ not included

These are your informal rules and the group would see someone who wants to treat the whole evening as a social event as disruptive. He/she would be breaking the group norms.

It is easy to identify formal groups. Management sets them up for a range of tasks, perhaps to oversee the installation and start-up of a new piece of machinery or to manage a relocation of desks during redecoration of the offices. It is harder to identify informal groups, but they are very important to all aspects of management.

While the group will have common goals, these goals may not be congruent with the objectives of the organisation. This is especially true of informal groups. For example, there may be a group of employees with young children. They may meet informally, over coffee breaks or lunch, and find that they have some common interests. If the organisation is winning more business but is reluctant to take on more employees, the informal group might start discussing any requests made for increased overtime and share a view that they do not want to work late. Members want to go home and see their children before they go to bed.

This is now an informal group with a goal that is different from that of the organisation. With the overtime being voluntary, they would choose not to work it. They would take comfort from the fact that the others in the informal group will not work overtime and, indeed, will not be happy if one of their group breaks with their norm. They will exert peer pressure to stop that individual from working later into the evening.

Management should recognise that these groups exist and manage them as much as they manage individuals.

5.1.1   Group formation

Groups are not formed ready to perform. While it is now a generally held view that a well formed group can produce results that exceed the sum of the individual members' efforts (social scientists call this **wholeism**), this is not true for all groups and is rarely the case for newly formed groups. In fact, it is probable that during the early stages of group formation, there will be a reduction in the quality or level of output compared with the output that the members could individually contribute.

Bruce Tuckman (1965) developed the theory of group development that is now most commonly held. He argued that when groups first form they spend some time getting to know each other. This is distracting from the task but nevertheless a crucial first step in forming a group. This stage is called **forming**.

The next stage is **storming**, where group members try different roles and 'sound out' their colleagues to develop an understanding of how the roles within the team will be shared out. It is likely that this will be subconscious. Most probably, the individual members will not even be thinking about roles, but will simply gravitate to roles that suit their personality. (Group roles are discussed later in this session.)

Next the group establishes who should take which role and establishes what the group goals should be. Remember that these may not be the goals that the organisation wants, and, indeed, it is likely that they will again be subconsciously agreed. The group also sets the rules by which it operates. This is the **norming** stage. For example, a group may have been set the task of maximising sales of a product that is in decline. When the group starts norming, it may be discussing limitations on the maximisation of sales of this product. It may even be unhappy to be set the task of promoting a declining product when other groups are working on new products. The group may then set an informal objective of minimising the damage to its positions should the product continue to decline. It may, perhaps, rehearse the arguments that it will put forward and even suggest that some research be carried out to support these arguments. Ostensibly it will try to maximise sales but internally its real goal now is to convince senior management that it has made the best of a bad situation.

Only after the norms (the rules) have been set and goals established does the group start **performing**. Ideas feed off the thoughts of others, enthusiasm grows and members enjoy the group's work. In turn, motivation increases and output improves. The group is thus performing. These four stages of group evolution are depicted in Figure 12.

Tuckman's evolution of groups	
Forming	The group is getting to know each other
Storming	Group members test each other and themselves to sort out roles
Norming	The members settle down to their roles, set group 'norms' and objectives
Performing	Finally, the group starts performing

Figure 12   The evolution of groups
(Source: Tuckman, 1965, p. 396)

Activity 5.1

Think about a group of which you have been a member. It may be a formal work group, a formal social group perhaps, or even an informal group. Write a few notes about how the group operated in each of Tuckman's group evolution stages.

Allow five minutes for this activity.

Feedback

You will probably have agreed with Tuckman that the group was not performing at its best until members had completed the norming stage. Management should therefore try to accelerate the group's progress through the first three stages. For the group to 'gel', for it to work effectively and have cohesion, the stages cannot be avoided, but if they can be shortened, then the overall efficiency will be improved.

One way to shorten the process is for key members to understand what is going on at these early stages of group formation, and to understand what the roles are towards which individuals are (usually subconsciously) moving. Much of the work on roles within groups is based on the work of Meredith Belbin (1981), which is discussed later.

5.1.2 Group cohesion

Groups that are more effective tend to have greater cohesion. However, what creates cohesion?

The six factors listed in the table below affect cohesion.

Factor	Cohesion is enhanced if:
The workflow	Work passes along from one worker to the next, for example, in a production line.
A shared outside threat	People band together to fend off an external threat.
Similarities in education and background	People share common backgrounds. It is possible to have cohesion if they do not, but it would be more difficult.
Similarities in the work	A group undertakes the same work or has similar targets and challenges.
Strongly desired goals	The group shares a common and very strong goal.
Interaction with group members	The group meets frequently, for example, as a result of working in the same office. Members get to know each other better and cohesion is enhanced. Groups formed from people from, say, different departments, can have cohesion but again, it is more challenging.

Managers can encourage cohesion by helping one or more of these factors to develop. For example, cohesion may be enhanced by adding a bonus for successful completion of a project or task, and thus strengthen the common goal.

Activity 5.2 ....

Spend a few minutes thinking about each factor above and how a manager might influence it to improve group cohesion.

Allow about 20 minutes for this activity.

Feedback ....

It is not always possible for the manager to influence every factor, but by understanding them, a manager can nurture the factor. For example, it would not be easy to change the production line where work passes from one group member to the next. However, when designing the line in the first place, it might have been possible to put people close enough for them to communicate with each other rather than putting them far apart and having batches of partly finished work delivered to them over a greater distance.

5.1.3 Roles within a group

High performing groups will have cohesion but it is not just the cohesion that makes them work: it is also the mix of individuals. A group needs a mix of skills or traits that results in individuals naturally filling the roles required for a group to work well. It is useful therefore to understand these roles.

Belbin (1981) identified eight different roles that people play in groups, as set out below.

Role	Attributes
Chairperson ('Chair')	Coordinates other group members to achieve the group goals. Stable Dominant Extrovert Good communicator Good at assessing ability of others *but* May not be very imaginative
Shaper	Pushes the group towards decisions and action. The Shaper will take an active part in the group (more so than the Chairperson). Dominant Impatient Extrovert *but* Anxious
Plant/Innovator	Often deliberately placed into a team to shake it up and to be an inspiration to the whole group. Dominant Very intelligent Introverted *but* Focuses on new ideas and the big picture Weak on detail
Monitor/Evaluator	Will be the group member who manages and evaluates the information. Objective analysis Sound judgement Capable of handling large quantities of data *but* Serious disposition
Team worker	Knows the group members well and works to support them, with the aim of achieving group goals. Not dominant Avoids confrontation
Resource investigator	Interacts with external sources of information, gathering data, ideas and gossip. Provides stimulation and imports ideas. Enthusiasm wanes quickly
Company worker	Transforms the group's ideas and strategies into achievable and logical objectives. Logical Practical *but* Dislikes sudden change
Completer/Finisher	Worries about completing the task. Checks accuracy and quality of the output. Detail oriented Diligent *but* May lose sight of the overall picture

(Source: derived from Belbin, 1981, *passim*)

Sometimes a person's personality will fit neatly into one of these roles but frequently people have elements of several different role characteristics.

While a 'chair' may be formally nominated when the group is established, most of these roles are established during the storming stage of the group evolution, in a subliminal way. The roles are not formally awarded to people. They just start to adopt them. It can often be the case that the officially nominated chair is not the 'real' chair who emerges from the group but instead a figurehead who may indeed adopt a different role within the group.

Belbin's work on roles in groups has been very influential in a wide variety of organisations.

It is getting the right mix of roles that is important to a successful group. A group consisting entirely of chair people or entirely of completer/finishers would be unlikely to operate smoothly. It would be more likely to fail to achieve its goal than a balanced group. If managers understand this and know their staff sufficiently well, they can put the right mix of people together, so increasing the probability that the group will be effective.

Belbin's description of roles is very useful, but it is not without limitations. You should not forget that it describes behaviours within groups and cannot measure personality traits in the individuals or even behaviour when acting alone. Further, the interaction with others can modify behaviour so an individual may behave slightly differently in different groups or when the group is working under different conditions, for example, when under stress. However, perhaps the most significant limitation is the cultural bias of Belbin. The theory was developed in Britain and focused on middle to senior level management. There is not enough empirical evidence to be certain that these behavioural traits would apply to a high performing group in a different cultural setting.

There is one other important characteristic that defines a group – its size. The people in the group need to be psychologically aware of each other in order to be effective, so normally a group would consist of no more than twelve people. Often formal committees consist of far more members than this. As a result, their deliberations can be long and drawn out. To address this, the real work may be carried out by smaller sub committees with the full committee being asked merely to note action taken or agree to recommendations which may already have been discussed in full with the committee chair.

While most people work in formal groups of some kind, many other kinds of groups operate at work on an informal basis, as you have seen. They do not enjoy the authority or recognition that formal groups have. They largely evolve out of individuals forming relationships with other people to pursue common interests. For example, people working together in an organisation might set up a lunch time chess club or wine club.

Activity 5.3   ....

Think of two groups to which you belong, one formal and one informal (they need not be work-related), and describe each of them according to the following group characteristics.

Characteristic	Formal group	Informal group
How many people belong to the group?		
What are the goals of the group?		
Does the group have an agreed identity and, if so, what are the signs (e.g., name, territory or rituals) that point to this?		
What are the group norms?		

Having described the groups, think about the ways in which you contribute to them and then finally, about how effective they are.

Using Belbin's classification, what role do you tend to adopt in the formal and informal groups you described above?

Allow about ten minutes for this activity.

Feedback ....

You probably found that you do not adopt the same role in both groups. In one you may find, for example, that you tend to act as a team worker in order to move the task forward. In the other you may find, for example, that you are able to indulge your skills as a resource investigator. You may feel more comfortable in one group than another. This is because our place in a group is not solely determined by our own preference, but often by other factors such as the skills or preferences of the other members, our technical abilities or, particularly in the formal group, our position in the company/firm structure. Some people have very strong preferences for one or two roles. Other people may be capable of filling several roles. However, people are likely to be more effective if they are given the chance to adopt their preferred role.

5.1.4   Conflict within groups

You have seen how groups can develop and become effective. Unfortunately, this is not always possible. Occasionally there will be some interpersonal conflict within a group which, if not managed properly, can start to detract from the efficiency of that group.

'Get lost, two's company, three's a shoal.'

However, not all conflict is bad. Conflict at work is often referred to as 'people playing games'. This can be a useful way of using conflict. One can look at it in two different ways. The first is as a win–lose scenario where one part of the group wins, and the other loses. This can never be positive for the outcome of the group as a whole and managers should try to contain such conflict. The second scenario is win–win, where both sides benefit from the conflict. For example, some of the group may be complacent but become stirred up by a seemingly antagonistic attitude displayed by other members. This creative tension causes everyone to reflect on their positions and develop new, better and more innovative solutions.

Activity 5.4 ....

However, if faced with a win–lose scenario, how should managers manage it? An imaginary group is used in the box below to explore what can happen, and how conflicts within a group might be managed.

> ### Group conflict in Carl's taxi service
>
> Carl is the manager of a taxi service, primarily taking clients to the airport and collecting them on their return. Three months ago he established a group to explore options and implement solutions for incremental remunerative work in the considerable wasted time his drivers spend waiting at airports between dropping off one client and collecting another. This is of interest to the drivers also as their pay is a mix of a daily rate and a percentage of the day's takings.
>
> Three of the drivers are group members, together with the office assistant, Jane, who is responsible for booking the diary. Jane is in her 40s and has worked for the firm for 12 years, since it was started by Carl's father. The three drivers in the group are Paul, a retired police officer of 53, who is looking to supplement his pension; Mary, a mother with school children; and Stephen, who is 26 and saving up to put a deposit down on a house. Carl chose these three drivers carefully to reflect a mix of the drivers' attitudes to the unusual working times that the job demands.
>
> Initially the group seemed to work well and some good ideas started to emerge. Members suggested using the waiting time to ferry people between airport hotels and the airport terminal. The group has now started the important implementation stage but Jane has asked to leave the group. When Carl asked her why, she explained that the constant sniping between Stephen and Paul is making the group work unpleasant and they never seem to be able to agree on what they should do next. Perhaps, more importantly, Carl noticed that the group's own deadlines for contacting airport hotels have slipped.
>
> Carl interviewed Paul and Stephen. Paul told him that Stephen appeared to want all of the airport hotel work for himself. Stephen said that Paul seemed to have no enthusiasm for the airport hotel work, being 'quite comfortable whiling away his time drinking coffee'.

This is the kind of situation that managers often have to deal with and the kind of breakdown in relationships that you may have come across at work. There is not just the issue of deteriorating working relationships to consider, but also a suggestion that it is having an effect upon the group's implementation programme. If the situation is allowed to continue, it is inevitable that performance will suffer, as other people are drawn into the issue just as Jane already appears to have been.

Think about this first from Stephen's point of view and suggest three reasons why he might see the situation as he does.

Now think about the situation from Paul's perspective and suggest three reasons why he might feel that Stephen is being unreasonable.

Allow five minutes for this activity.

Feedback ....

Stephen may feel that Paul is not a good team player and that his lack of drive is endangering this potentially lucrative new work and will impact adversely on his own earnings. There are many reasons why Paul may feel antagonistic towards Stephen, and they probably stem from the fact that he sees Stephen as a threat to his potential earnings, to his 'comfort zone' and to his position as 'elder statesman' of the group.

The fact that we can find reasons for their attitudes and behaviour does not mean that it is therefore acceptable. Both Stephen and Paul are relying to some extent upon stereotypical assumptions that they are making about each other.

The case study demonstrates that different members of a group may have different views of reality or **conceptual maps**.

Many problems between people occur because they do not share the same view of reality. Our own particular view of the world is shaped by our culture, personal values and upbringing, and the experiences we have in life. As we become older, we tend to reinforce our particular version of reality by refusing to consider or accept information that might contradict it. Researchers have used the idea of the conceptual map to describe the way in which individuals seek to understand and represent the world and themselves within it. Our conceptualisations of reality, or at least those parts of it that we find meaningful or interesting, shape the way we react to and work with others.

If relationships between people are beginning to cause problems, as in the case study, you should not assume that the individuals concerned are deliberately being difficult. The problem here has much to do with the fact that the individuals do not share the same view of reality. For at least one member of this group, the reality is that pushy young men want to displace mature experience. Stephen's reality, on the other hand, may well include a particular view of middle-aged men. In each case, such stereotypical views will inform their holders' reaction to situations that present themselves.

Members of a group may not share the same goals and their personal goals may differ from those of the organisation.

In the case study it is possible that personal goals and individual values have become more important than those of the group. Mary may not want to work the longer hours that may be associated with the airport hotel business, preferring to arrive home earlier to spend time with her children. Paul may be willing to do the work but it is Stephen who is eager to do it in order to build up his deposit for a house. Jane possibly sees little for her in the group objectives. She would not see any incremental income, and, perhaps, this has shaped her request to leave the group.

A manager cannot assume that just because certain people find themselves working together in a group, they will automatically work towards the same organisational goals.

One way of explaining human behaviour is by recognising that for much of the time at work we are conscious of the role we need to play and are acting the part. People tend to behave according to the role expected of them. For example, research has shown that if the performance of children in school is predicted to improve it will tend to do so. Similarly, if teachers' expectations of pupils are low, their work or behaviour is likely to deteriorate.

5.1.5   Dealing with difference

Recognising and valuing diversity in a team can be empowering. Two things that you can conclude, therefore, about working with people are that they will be different from you and that you cannot make assumptions about their behaviour. What may seem strange or disruptive behaviour to you may seem straightforward and normal to them. Also your own behaviour, which seems perfectly reasonable to you, may appear completely inappropriate to others.

It is, of course, not just people's behaviour that tells us that they are different from us. Everyone is aware of difference, for example, difference in race, religion, gender, height, weight and so on. The problems arise when this awareness of difference is accompanied by stereotyping. It is often hard to avoid this as negative images about certain differences may have become part of a person's conceptual map. Difference should be valued if only because variety in groups gives more resources, solutions to problems, and so on.

Stereotypes may be deeply embedded in individuals' versions of reality. The first step is for them to recognise that they may be making assumptions about people unjustly because, for example, they have a stereotypical view about some aspect of their behaviour, cultural background or appearance.

5.1.6   Preventing conflict

Clearly the most effective strategy is to prevent conflict from arising in the first place. Some of the ideas associated with effective management that you have studied in the previous sessions will be helpful. The list below will remind you of some of them.

- Be aware that others do not share your view of reality.
- Involve others in planning and decision making where possible.
- Try to understand what motivates people and what their individual needs might be.
- Be aware of the importance to individuals and groups of regular feedback so that they can evaluate progress.
- Value individual difference.
- Look for win – win situations.
- Create an environment where effective group work is possible.

5.2   What is a team?

Often the terms 'group' and 'team' are used interchangeably but there are important, if subtle, differences. All teams are groups, but not all groups are teams and therefore all that has been said about groups applies equally to teams, but a team has something more: a team is a particular sort of group. Like a group, a team will have a common goal and identity. What distinguishes a team is really its focus combined with the way in which the group of individuals work together to achieve that focus. In doing so, they achieve more than they could achieve individually.

Management will attempt to build teams for particular projects or tasks, although for a group to develop into a team there are certain prerequisites in that:

- team members need to have frequent and regular interactions with each other
- the activities of the team members need to be coordinated and synergistic
- the skills and competences of the team members will tend to be complementary and self-reinforcing
- there needs to be a high level of collaboration between the members of the team.

Activity 5.5 ....

Think about a successful team in the field of sport. Quickly write down the words you would associate with such a team.

Allow five minutes for this activity.

Feedback ....

Your list might include words such as commitment, organisation, shared objectives, mutual respect, high level of skill, results, rewards, tactics and individual tasks. Looking at this list and comparing it with the characteristics of a group, which were covered earlier, you should see that a team is more dynamic and more organised than a group needs to be. Also, a team might operate in situations where there is ambiguity or uncertainty about the outcome yet remain cohesive because of the common strong belief in the objective.

Simply putting people into a group and calling them a team does not mean that they will actually work like one and yet, when management deliberately asks a group of individuals to work together, it is invariably seeking to construct a team: something that is more effective than the sum of the individuals.

It is now time to take a look at what can be done to make groups into effective teams.

5.3 Turning groups into effective teams

There are two kinds of ways in which groups can be turned into effective teams. The first thing to check is the contextual factors, that is, the givens with which the group has to work. The second is the way in which the group manages itself, namely the internal factors.

Contextual factors

Size and composition. In a work environment, a group with more than twelve members is likely to be too big to form a really effective team. Hence, a small group of like-minded people might, on the face of it, seem ideal. However, with a small group there is a narrower range of skills upon which to draw. If the group is homogeneous and its members share the same values and have a similar version of reality, there may be less conflict, but there could also be less of the creative tension that can produce effective and innovative solutions.

Task. The team will respond better to a clear and unambiguous task, which is seen to be important as well as challenging.

Resources. The resources available to the team must be adequate for the task. One of the quickest ways of reducing morale is to make it difficult or impossible to complete the task because of lack of resources. Resources in this context mean finance, equipment, training, skills or information.

External recognition. From what you learned about motivation in Session 4, you will understand how important external recognition is for both individuals and teams. The important research carried out by Mayo in the 1920s and 1930s, which you encountered earlier in this unit, showed that workers are more productive if they feel that they are valued by management.

Internal factors

Leadership. The way in which a team is led can be very important. If there is to be a designated team leader, then the leadership must be acceptable to and accepted by the members of the group if it is to perform well.

Task and process functions. **Task functions** refer to deciding what is to be done. **Process functions** are about how things are to be done. Task functions tend to be the ones that receive attention in teams, largely because work needs to be carried out in a systematic way in order to complete the task. Typical task functions are shown in the box below.

Common task functions

Proposing/initiating	Proposing ideas and courses of action that are relevant to the task
Building	Developing other people's proposals
Diagnosing	Analysing what is wrong or identifying the cause of a particular situation
Giving and seeking information	Giving and seeking information that is relevant to the task
Evaluating	Evaluating the merits of particular proposals and outcomes
Decision making	Contributing to decisions on a particular process or course of action

The process (or maintenance) functions, on the other hand, often get overlooked. They focus upon the people in the group and are about creating a working environment in which the contributions of individuals are respected and encouraged and the people themselves feel involved and valued. Typical process functions are shown in the following box.

Common process (or maintenance) functions

Gate keeping	Opening – attempting to involve others in discussions. Closing – attempting to control others, or cutting them out of discussions
Encouraging	Being friendly, supportive and responsive to other people by verbal or non-verbal means
Conflict resolution	Being prepared to acknowledge and deal with conflict
Giving feedback	Giving constructive feedback on people's contributions
Dealing with feelings	Recognising and acknowledging people's feelings
Looking after physical needs	Meeting people's physical needs, for example, by providing adequate amenities, refreshments, and so on

It is clear that some of these maintenance or process functions are important simply because they relate to the motivational needs of individuals. Perhaps the most important aspect of motivation, however, for people working in teams is that the overall aim or goal must be clear and must be valued by them. If this is not the case, then group or team members are likely to put their own interests before those of the group or team.

The environment. One factor that has not yet been considered is the environment in which teams operate, that is, in the sense of the physical location. You will remember from the Hawthorne studies that the physical surroundings in which work takes place clearly have an influence upon productivity, but not necessarily in the way you would expect. Physical proximity helps interaction and cooperation. However, the location does not necessarily have to be luxurious and comfortable.

5.4 The fifth stage in group formation

You should note this final stage of adjourning in this influential typology.

The stages of group formation you have seen are forming, storming, norming and performing. However, groups do not go on for ever. There is an important fifth stage that follows once the group's purpose has been achieved. This is referred to as **adjourning**.

If a group has been particularly successful, its members will feel a strong affiliation to it. They will, after all, have invested a huge amount of personal energy in the work of the group, identified with the group's goals and adopted group norms. Remember, too, that for many people, working in a group can help to fulfil strong social needs. It is no wonder then that when the group is disbanded these people feel a sense of loss. They need to be allowed the opportunity to 'mourn' the passing of the group. It has been found that, if this is denied, people are less willing to commit themselves in the same way to a new group, fearing the disbanding of the new group could bring the risk of similar pain in the future.

Just as groups do not go on indefinitely, group composition changes from time to time as people leave to work elsewhere or are asked to join the group because they have particular skills, which are needed. When this happens, the group effectively becomes a new group and the process of group formation will be repeated to some extent while the change is absorbed. Eventually, the group will reach the performing stage and work effectively.

Summary

Groups and teams are critical to the operation of any organisation. The way in which groups are formed and the way in which individual members of a group may behave were explored as an introduction to managing groups. Teams are special groups and managers must pay as much attention to their formation as they do to any group.

To help you to understand how managers can influence group and team development, the session looked at the key barrier to group effectiveness, namely, conflict. Of course, some conflict can be helpful: it is called creative tension. However, there are some negative conflicts which must be managed. Finally, the way in which managers can enhance the performance of a team was considered in terms of their need to focus on contextual and internal factors.

SESSION 6 Training and development within the organisation

Introduction

Upon completion of Session 6 you are expected to be able to:

- explain the importance of learning in the workplace
- describe theories of how people learn
- describe the role of the human resources department (HRD) and individual managers in the learning process
- describe and list the benefits of the training and development process
- explain the importance of performance appraisal
- describe and explain the benefits of an effective appraisal process.

Employees are recruited to contribute to the organisation's objectives. It follows, therefore, that there must be systems in place to assess the extent of that contribution and to promote continuing high performance. Several techniques contribute to making this possible, including developing people through training and monitoring performance.

6.1 The importance of learning in the workplace

© Cartoonstock.com

It is useful to think about why many organisations devote so much resource to training and development, before considering how they do it. First, there are two activities to help you think about the advantages of training and development. The feedback from these activities provides some valuable learning points, but do attempt the activities yourself before reading the feedback. Training and development have been touched on in a number of sessions in this unit, so you will probably already have some good ideas.

Activity 6.1   ....

Make a list of the advantages of a good training and development plan for the organisation and for the individual.

Allow about ten minutes for this activity.

Feedback   ....

You probably came up with an extensive list of both, but here are our thoughts.

Cultural benefits

On joining an organisation, a person knows that he/she is at the start of what is likely to be a steep learning curve. First, the daily tasks that are part of the job need to be learned as well as the names and locations of people with whom he/she needs to communicate in order to perform his/her tasks. The working environment and the culture of the organisation have to be understood, and the important formal and informal groups worked out. Settling into the 'way we do things here' is an essential prerequisite to mastering the new role. Proper induction can reduce the time it takes for new employees to be assimilated into the organisation's culture.

It is not only new joiners who can benefit culturally: organisations operating across international boundaries can develop training programmes better to integrate the wider group. Organisations which acquire another organisation may use training and development as one way in which to accelerate integration of the new organisation's workforce.

Operating costs

Most business organisations have a primary objective of maximising shareholder value. The cost of their operations is therefore a critical factor. The benefits of induction training for new recruits were discussed above. This, of course, helps to make them effective contributors to the organisation at an earlier stage. However, training can also aid the productivity of all employees, reduce wastage and lower the cost of managing the workforce which will then be better able to work without direct supervision.

The effectiveness of teams can be enhanced or accelerated through the development stages, by the use of appropriate training.

Enhancement of the quality of the workforce

The workforce is a key resource. This theme will be revisited throughout this session. Developing the skill set of employees will:

- increase the flexibility and adaptability of individuals to tackle new tasks or to deputise for colleagues when needed
- reduce staff turnover by offering more intrinsic rewards to staff, and making their careers more rewarding
- improve the motivation of the workforce and thereby increase its overall efficiency
- assist with succession planning to ensure that the workforce will continue to be capable of meeting the organisational needs.

Change management

It is not just people new to an organisation who need to learn. Organisations may adopt a new policy demanding new skills and making new demands on staff or, indeed, the organisation may go through a period of transformational change itself requiring employees to adapt with it. A well designed training and development programme can help to explain the change and why it is needed, and equip the workforce with the appropriate skills.

Benefits to the individual

The individual gains the benefit of enhancing his/her skills and feels more capable of completing his/her job. There is also a Hawthorne effect, as discussed in Session 1. The fact that management considers the individual worth training will motivate that individual. Other benefits to employees are less tangible. Their status can be enhanced, they can also widen their network within the organisation and, possibly, join informal groups (see Session 5).

The previous activity showed that there are many benefits of training and development, but how can they be made effective?

Activity 6.2   ....

People working in all organisations and undertaking all functions will benefit from training at some stage. Consider the following roles and list the areas of training that may be appropriate to them.

> Mohamed has worked at a power generation plant for over ten years. He is 53 and expects to continue in his job until retirement. His actual role is in general maintenance where he is the foreman of a four person group responsible for maintaining the ancillary buildings and perimeter fencing. Mohamed has the opportunity to move to the power plant maintenance team but this would mean not being a group foreman, a role he enjoys, as the new post would be a more senior one. He is comfortable where he is and simply wants to stay there.

> Julia runs a local travel agency, part of a chain of six agencies covering the region. She has one permanent member of staff working for her and a number of part time people to cover the peak season and weekends. Julia is 27. While she loves the work she is doing, managing the part time staff can prove troublesome. One of the part time members, a young man straight out of school, has proved quite disruptive. His timekeeping is poor and he tends to spend more time chatting to his co-workers than dealing with customers. Julia's boss, Nigel, has been monitoring Julia as a potential candidate to run the chain's premier agency but he has some concerns about her ability to manage staff.

Spend about ten minutes on this activity.

Feedback   ....

No doubt you thought of plenty of training opportunities for Julia, not just in terms of people management but also of more general management skills that could be developed to help her become even more suitable to run the premier outlet. However, what about Mohamed? He seems quite happy where he is and there are no apparent performance issues. Managers will frequently come across fully competent staff members who are content to continue where they are. You can probably find some training that would be suitable for him – perhaps some technical training on new maintenance equipment. However, the process of encouraging him to develop himself becomes as important as the training itself.

There is not just one way that people learn, and finding the right way to teach them will encourage them to participate in the training. Let us look at some theory about how we learn and how a line manager might better map the type of training to the individual.

Now that you have given some thought to the advantages of learning and development within the workplace, some of the theory supporting it will be explored.

6.2 The learning process

In the first half of the twentieth century, training the workforce was quite simple: we learned 'on the job'. 'Sitting next to Nellie' was the catchphrase used for this type of training. If, after a period of time, an employee's performance was not deemed to be satisfactory, the employee might be asked to leave. Alternatively, the individual might be feeling so demotivated because he/she felt ill equipped to do what was being required that he/she would move on to another job with another firm. David Kolb (1984) provides what is probably the most widely accepted description of the situational learning process.

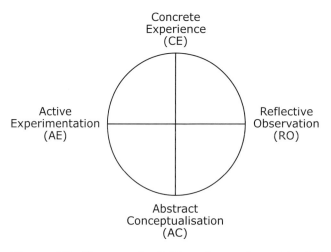

Kolb's experiential learning cycle is another important framework you are likely to come across whenever you address learning in the workplace.

Figure 13 The experiential learning cycle and basic learning styles (Source: Adapted from Kolb, 1984, p. 42.)

Within experiential learning theory, learning is defined as 'the process whereby knowledge is created through the transformation of experience. Knowledge results from the combination of grasping and transforming experience' (Kolb, 1984, p. 41). Within Figure 13, there are two opposed modes of *grasping* experience – **concrete experience** and **abstract conceptualisation**. Correspondingly, also within Figure 13, there are two dialectically related modes of *transforming* experience – **reflective observation** and **active experimentation**. According to the four stage learning cycle depicted in Figure 13, concrete experience acts as a basis for reflections which are transformed into abstract concepts. In turn, the latter can result in new implications for action which can be evaluated and so serve as guides in creating new experiences.

In other words, we benefit from concrete experience when we do something and learn that something works, or does not. Accordingly, we use concrete experience to validate and test abstract concepts. Perhaps something does not go quite as well as we had hoped and we decide to spend some time on reflective observation, watching how others tackle the task and evaluating their outcomes. The third stage is the formation of abstract conceptualisation in which the individual needs to build a framework in his or her mind about what has been learned. This will allow him/her to test the implications of concepts in new situations – active experimentation which forms the final stage of the cycle.

Applying Kolb's model to how a builder might learn

A builder, new to the trade, attempts to join two pieces of wood with a screw. One piece of wood splits so he tries again, but this time drills a pilot hole in the first piece of wood and this works. He reflects on what happened and has learned that by drilling a hole first, he can prevent the wood splitting. He will not make that mistake again. During his coffee break he discusses this experience with a colleague. The colleague explains that wood has strength across the grain but will split down the grain quite easily, and by drilling the pilot hole he can avoid putting too much stress along the grain. The builder now has an abstract conceptualisation of what has happened that he will apply to working with wood in a broader context than just joining two pieces.

The next day the builder is asked to fix a wooden door-frame inside a brick opening. He is now joining wood to brick but he can apply his learning from yesterday and drill pilot holes before screwing the wood to the wall. He is undertaking active experimentation.

The above box described a simple example and the builder will not have realised that he was working through Kolb's four stages of learning. The concept also applies to more complex learning situations. However, not everyone prefers to learn in the same way. Kolb, working with Roger Fry (Kolb and Fry, 1975, pp. 38–48) recognised this and argued that different people will experience stronger learning at different stages. If the stages that are most favourable to an individual can be understood, then the learning outcome can be maximised. For example, some people learn better by watching others and then experimenting themselves. They prefer the reflective observation and active experimentation stages. Other people may prefer to get stuck in and then to think about the process that they tried. They prefer concrete experience and abstract conceptualisation. Kolb believed that people would tend to favour two of his stages and he developed a framework of learning styles around this assumption. He identified four styles, as described below.

Converger (Abstract conceptualisation and active experimentation). Individuals favouring this style tend to be strong on practical application and have a strong focus on tasks. They learn by doing things and are good at finding further uses for their solutions, and the solutions found by others. Their interest is limited beyond the immediate task.

Diverger (Concrete experimentation and reflective observation). Individuals using this style tend to be imaginative people, good at generating a range of potential solutions to a problem and seeing things from different angles. Their preferred learning style is to watch other people doing things and suggest improvements. They tend to be social people and work well in groups. They are also interested in matters beyond the immediate problem.

Assimilator (Abstract conceptualisation and reflective observation). Assimilators are good at developing abstract or theoretical models and also have strong logical reasoning skills. They prefer to learn from research and can gather a wide range of information and organise it into a useful framework. They are more likely to be interested in abstract concepts than people.

Accommodator (Concrete experience and active experimentation). Accommodators love doing things and solving problems intuitively. They are good at taking someone else's theoretical approach to solving a problem and making it work. They are good at facing urgent, immediate problems, but will tend to take more risk than other learning styles.

Mumford (1996, p. 6) developed a different set of learning styles which map quite closely on to Kolb's four learning stages. Their learning styles are activist, reflector, theorist and pragmatist, as shown below.

Comparison of ways of learning

Mumford's typology of learners	Kolb's learning stage	Attributes
Activist	Concrete experience	Likes to solve problems immediately Acts before thinking Likes new challenges Flexible Easily bored
Reflector	Reflective observation	Gathers information before starting Listens to other views and suggestions Prefers to work alone Plans carefully and does not like unplanned situations Sets their own pace, usually slow and cautious
Theorist	Abstract conceptualisation	Analytical and logical Objective and rational Aims for perfection Uncomfortable with uncertainty or subjectivity (so does not like to consider new approaches)
Pragmatist	Active experimentation	Applies theory to practice Only enjoys learning things that are immediately useful Eager to tackle problems immediately Uncomfortable without guidelines and firm timetables Enjoys coaching and feedback; likes immediate recognition

Both Mumford's and Kolb's models provide some food for thought. However, the main criticism of their models is that they are theoretical. Do people consistently learn in the styles described? Do people pass through each of Kolb's four stages? Certainly the empirical evidence to support this is not extensive. Despite these concerns the models are informative, but how can managers use them?

Activity 6.3 ....

Think about your own preference for learning. Can you identify your way of learning with one of Kolb's or Mumford's learning styles? Can you think of a colleague or friend who has approached learning from a different angle? If so, can you identify his/her learning style?

If you are managing a group of people with different learning styles, what might this mean for the way you approach their training and development?

Spend about ten minutes on this activity.

Feedback ....

Managers should try to encourage individuals to complete all stages of the learning process, but need to recognise that different individuals will spend more time on different stages. The danger in not encouraging all stages is that the learning is not reinforced or is not made fully transferable to fresh situations. Remember, however, that it really is not a case of 'one size fits all' and managers should be flexible in matching a training approach to an individual's learning style.

6.3 Structuring learning within an organisation

6.3.1 The roles of line managers and human resource departments

During the second half of the twentieth century, firms slowly began to realise that training and developing staff members could play an important part in the success of the business. Britain had seen a notable deterioration in its comparative competitiveness and there was a clear need to enhance management training. More recently, organisations have found that having a good, systematic training and development programme not only improves individual and organisational performance, but also ensures that the company attracts and retains good recruits.

The role of managers has therefore broadened to include the training and development of their staff. They have a human resource role that is an important component of their job description. In this they are supported by a human resource department (HRD) but the principal responsibility for staff development normally lies with the line manager who needs to recognise training requirements. Managers will set individual objectives for their staff when carrying out annual appraisals. Training and development requirements are usually also discussed at this juncture, as you will see later in this session.

Human resource management has an increasingly important strategic role, recognising that people are a key resource. Large organisations will normally appoint a Human Resources Director who, ideally, will be a member of the management board and will be seen as being as important as the Finance and Marketing Directors. When business strategy is being formulated, the HR Director will consider how to develop existing employees as well as how to recruit talented new people. However, having existing staff with the skill sets required has distinct advantages, as outlined below.

- They are already 'insiders'. They are part of the organisation and know its culture, its policies and its procedures.

- They are flexible. Teams can be put together quickly to tackle urgent projects and then disbanded and people sent back to their original roles if the project proves unattractive, for example, if the organisation is contemplating a takeover of another organisation which does not go ahead.

- They have known competences. No matter how good a recruitment programme is, the organisation cannot form a full opinion of new recruits until they have been with the organisation for a period. When there is a new project, this initial period can be crucial.

Not only can training contribute to the organisation's ability to achieve its objectives, but it can transform the lives and prospects of the individuals who benefit from it. Many prospective employees will judge whether to work for an organisation partly on the basis of the opportunities for advancement it affords them. A significant proportion of those opportunities is provided by training and development.

Finance directors may argue that the decision to spend resources – time and money – on training and developing people should be a rational one, comparable with the decision to invest, for example, in the latest capital equipment. Training and development will tend to increase the productivity of the individual or group being trained, and can be extremely motivating, so investment in these activities may be desirable to the extent that the costs incurred will be less than the value of the increased performance expected. There is, however, no guarantee that this will be the case. Not all training will improve the productivity or flexibility of the organisation. In fact, training can lead to employees being poached by competitors before the organisation has had a chance to recoup the training costs.

Once senior management has established the strategic staffing needs of the organisation in terms of what is required to pursue the organisation's strategy, these needs will be reflected in the training and development plan (notably in the job descriptions and job specifications) and in the recruitment plan.

6.4 Analysing training needs

How does the manager know the type of training that an individual needs? The manager could simply draw on his/her own experience and the performance of the individual, and thereby build a picture of what is needed to develop the performance of that individual. However, would this be properly aligned with the organisation? Would it be targeted to develop the individual for other future roles, perhaps in a different team?

If the manager has the time, he/she may make a reasonable job of developing a training and development programme, but it is preferable to centralise much of this broad planning into the human resources department. That department is better able to take a holistic view of the organisation's training and development needs in order for it to achieve its strategic objectives. The HRD can build into job specifications the specific competences needed across the pool of staff to meet these strategic objectives.

Figure 14 outlines the stages in establishing training needs.

Training needs analysis

Figure 14   A diagrammatic representation of the training needs analysis process

6.4.1   Job description

How does a human resources department use the training needs analysis to establish the learning needs of individuals? The process starts by describing the functions and competences of an ideal employee and, from these, a template can be drawn up which can be used to develop employees.

Through interviewing job holders and management, as well as through observing how jobs are performed, the HRD develops a detailed description of a job which is broken down into:

- *tasks* which are the individual actions required, such as a machinist having the task of operating the lathe
- *duties* which are the objectives or desired outcomes, for example, the machinist may be required to make spindles for electric generators
- *responsibilities* which are the people and physical resources that the job holder is accountable for.

Activity 6.4   ....

Consider your own job (past or present) or, if you have never had a job, think about one you have read about. This will probably be within an organisation, but it may be something you do on your own. Now complete the following table. Obviously you will have a few duties with many tasks, and some tasks may be repeated for different duties. Three tasks per duty are shown, but you may have more. Next describe the responsibilities associated with each task. What human resources, budgets or equipment are you responsible for? Remember to do this for the ideal job holder, which you may not yet be but may aspire to being. Of course, this is confidential to you so do be honest with yourself.

Duties	Tasks required to complete duties	Responsibilities
	Task 1	Responsibility 1
Duty 1	Task 2	Responsibility 2
	Task 3	Responsibility 3

This job analysis activity will be used again in the next session.

Allow five minutes for this activity.

Feedback ....

Duties tend to be activities, such as undertaking to do something, completing a task, ensuring that something is done, providing, advising, arranging, authorising and so on.

Resources for which you may be responsible may include accounts staff, for example, if you happen to be in an accounting supervisory or managerial role. In such a role, you would be likely to have budgetary authority up to a certain level and to make specific types of expenditure necessary to perform your role.

6.4.2 Job specification

Job specification involves the identification of specific attributes that are desirable or essential in an ideal job holder. Certain skills, knowledge and qualifications may be necessary. The desirable attributes can be developed by training, but there are always some core attributes that the job holder has to have already in order to complete the job which are the essential attributes.

The three main areas are identified below.

- *Knowledge,* which covers general educational and professional training and development. An accountant may need to be qualified with an acceptable professional accountancy body.

- *Skills* which are job-specific skills needed to complete the job. The accountant must be numerate and, perhaps, competent at using specific types of accounting software.

- *Competences,* which are the overall attributes and behaviours needed to perform the job. An accountant needs to be diligent and able to work alone without supervision.

Each of these should be classified as essential or desirable. You can see from this that there are subtle, but important, differences in the way in which the terms education, training and development are interpreted. In reality, these areas tend to overlap but it is useful to differentiate the terms when considering a training and development programme. These areas are discussed below.

Education	This is normally the education received at school or university, and a university degree may be specified for some managerial jobs. However, education is much wider: it is general rather than specific to a job or organisation and is usually therefore transferable from organisation to organisation. Education frequently continues during employment. Individuals may wish to continue their own education by taking an Open University degree. They may undertake professional vocational training such as an accountancy qualification. Education may also be provided by the employer such as providing language training for sales staff who have to visit clients abroad.
Training	This will normally be job-specific, training individuals to carry out the tasks needed to complete the duties associated with their job.
Development	This is a composite of both education and training to ensure that employees have or gain the education needed to provide a broadly based platform of knowledge (or perhaps an ability to analyse a problem critically). It also ensures that the individual is skilled at the specific tasks needed to perform the activities relevant to his/her job.

Information about the job and the abilities that a competent job holder needs can now be passed to the line manager so that he/she can use this information to assess the actual job holder during performance reviews. From this comparison it is possible to establish the gap between the member of staff and the ideal job holder. How the line manager measures an individual's competences is a significant topic in itself. Before moving on to this, you will see how all this work can be pulled together to produce a training and development plan.

As with performance reviews, a training and development plan is primarily the responsibility of the individual's line manager, rather than that of the Human Resources department. Training, as indicated in the table above, is normally job specific, in that it involves training individuals to carry out the tasks needed to complete the duties connected with their job. By way of contrast, development encompasses both education and development itself and aims to provide the individual with a broad basis of knowledge or perhaps to develop a more abstract ability, such as critical reasoning. However, in addition to this, such a training and development plan will need to ensure that the individual attains the necessary skills so as to be able to carry out the activities specific to his/her job. A final key feature of a training and development plan is that it will usually include approximate timings during the coming performance review year for such training and development activities, perhaps with the addition of details of specific events or courses that the individual member of staff could attend.

Activity 6.5   ....

You can now build on the job analysis that you did in Activity 6.4 and prepare a job specification.

For each task you identified, list the knowledge, skills and competences that are needed to do the task.

Spend about five minutes on this activity.

Feedback   ....

The knowledge, skills and competences that you have identified will be specific to your job, but you are likely to have included:
- analytical skills
- motivational and social skills
- attitudes and behaviours appropriate to the tasks (including personal qualities, for example, a customer service manager will need to appear friendly and approachable)
- education and training needed to complete the tasks.

6.4.3   Performance review

Performance review of an individual member of staff is usually primarily the responsibility of the line manager. Such a review will normally be carried out at regular intervals, usually at least once per year but sometimes more often, with the main aim of assessing the individual concerned. This will usually include an assessment of that individual's knowledge with respect to his/her job, particular relevant skills and competences.

6.4.4   Gap analysis

Information about the job and the abilities that a competent job holder needs can now be passed to the line manager so that he/she can use this information to assess the actual job holder during performance reviews. It is then possible to establish the gap between the member of staff and the ideal job holder. Of course, the intention is not to portray individual employees as sub-standard. Indeed, that would be likely to elicit a negative response from the workforce. Instead, the intention is to enhance continuously the abilities of the workforce. Managers must be careful to describe the training and development programme in this way.

This analysis is important for developing people for the next job, for promotion or simply to become flexible enough to provide cover during the absence of colleagues or to meet unforeseen challenges. The duties and skills or competences of employees can be enhanced in order to meet the organisation's needs.

A plan can therefore be devised for the individual's training and development that will help him/her to develop. It should also help realign the individual, and therefore eventually the entire workforce, with the changing competences needed by the organisation.

6.4.5   Competence assessment

Competences have been mentioned briefly, but what exactly are they and why are they so important to the training and development of individuals?

In the present climate of seemingly continual transformational change, management must constantly be thinking about and preparing for the future. Business strategy is likely to be flexible to take into account future uncertainties. The emphasis on training and development therefore has to reflect this need for flexibility and has started to shift from the tasks employees do now to the way they do the job, that is, their attitudes, skills and behaviours are seen as important as well.

This trend is international, though it has been particularly noticeable in the UK where governments and employers have been concerned about increasing the vocational relevance of the education and training carried out by schools and institutions of further and higher education. Competence-based approaches to assessing the training needs of individuals have four distinct areas, as set out below.

- They concern the abilities and behaviours required to perform specified roles and tasks to the standards required in employment.

- They focus on what staff and managers can do – their behaviour and its outcomes – rather than their experience and skills or the education they require.

- They are concerned with generic work roles, that is, broad classes of jobs, rather than particular positions.

- They are research-based, aiming to replace arbitrariness and subjectivity with empirically validated and tested formulations.

You may be forgiven for saying: 'Well, OK, but first, what type of behaviour are we talking about and how do we measure it?' You should find that the following activity will help you to answer these questions.

Activity 6.6 ....

Imagine that the behaviours in the following table are those that are specified for your boss in his/her job. Think carefully about each behaviour. Read the supporting range statement, then rate your boss on a 1–100 per cent scale. A score of 100 per cent means that his/her competences are outstanding! If you do not have a boss, think about a supervisor you have known through work or even through a work of fiction, such as a film or television series.

Competences and behaviours

Competence	Range statement	Score
Interpersonal skills	Uses open and probing questions, summaries, paraphrasing, etc., to understand the ideas, concepts and feelings of another; can comprehend events, issues, problems, opportunities from the viewpoint of another person.	
Managing interaction	Involves others and is able to build cooperative teams in which group members feel valued and empowered and have shared goals.	
Impact	Uses a variety of positive methods to gain support for ideas, strategies and values.	
Presentation	Presents ideas clearly, with ease and interest so that others understand what is being communicated.	
Proactive orientation	Structures the task for the team; implements plans and ideas; takes responsibility for all aspects of the situation.	
Achievement orientation	Possesses high internal work standards and sets ambitious yet attainable goals; wants to do things better, to improve, to be more effective and efficient; measures progress against targets.	

Spend about ten minutes on this activity.

Feedback ....

How did your actual or imaginary boss score on these competences? Did you find it helpful to use the detailed range above rather than simply terms such as 'interpersonal skills'? Also, having to give these competences a numerical value is likely to have helped crystallise your opinions.

The analysis approach to training needs has important benefits. It is systematic, and so helps to prevent both the line manager and the job holder forgetting to think about key parts of the job. However, this approach works best with well defined jobs that require specific skills or techniques that can be reliably cultivated among people who are willing to acquire them. There are problems that may complicate the use of this approach, examples of which are given below.

- If the work is unstructured and rather fluid, it will be more difficult to break it down into discrete tasks. In addition, in a small firm, the roles will be less specialised and defined.

- The skills and knowledge required may not be obvious from lists of the tasks and duties.

- It may not be easy to train a person in the abilities required (although his/her abilities can be enhanced or developed over time, to some extent).
- People who offer particular skills may resent being told that they are 'deficient' in others and need training.

In an ideal organisational world, each and every job would have an up-to-date skills and attitude description that could be used by job holders to evaluate their own individual training requirements.

6.5 Performance appraisal

Performance appraisal involves the review and appraisal by a line manager usually of an employee's performance against previously agreed objectives. It is easy to measure performance against quantifiable performance requirements, such as achieving a certain percentage cost reduction or ensuring a given percentage utilisation of a machine. However, moving into a broader competence-based assessment brings increasing difficulty in measuring performance. How are behaviours measured? This point has been debated for many years in organisations and in the academic world but inevitably it requires a degree of subjectivity. Here are some approaches, using an OU tutor as an example.

- The tutor can 'self-report'. For example, he/she may look at the Tutor Competences form and give a rating for each competence of, say, 50 per cent or 60 per cent.
- The tutor could ask for students' responses (**upward appraisal** or **customer appraisal**). An upward appraisal is where subordinates appraise their boss. However, as students you really are the tutor's 'customers'. Obtaining feedback from customers is becoming increasingly common: they are, after all, the parties who really matter.
- The tutor could request that another tutor look at his/her work, attend his/her tutorials, and then give an assessment (**peer assessment**).
- When the tutor's next staff appraisal is due, his/her line manager could be asked for help in developing competences so that a higher level can be attained.
- A **'360-degree' appraisal** can be conducted. With this approach, the tutor's subordinates (if any), their peers (fellow tutors) and their line manager all have input to the appraisal process, as well as their customers (students), perhaps.

The appraisal would provide a picture of how the tutor is perceived by others. This is a valuable type of feedback, but some people would argue that ratings by subordinates and self are lenient and undifferentiated. The reasons for this are not difficult to understand. If you were asked to assess your manager, you might be reluctant to give a low rating, because this is a person who may, at a future date, recommend your promotion! Your work colleagues may likewise prefer not to rate you at too low a level because you are a member of the team, and, perhaps, a friend as well as a colleague.

However difficult it is, the formal performance review is critical. It provides an opportunity for reflection on past performance and the identification of future goals (by both the line manager and the appraisee), along with the support required to achieve them. It also allows formal discussion and feedback. All too often communication on performance becomes confused when it is carried out on an ad hoc basis. Try to remember the last time you received feedback outside of the formal appraisal. Did you find it short and lacking in description? Perhaps you felt it was a 'throwaway' comment by your line manager. Without the formal setting, informal appraisal is frequently poorly considered and badly communicated.

Appraisals lend themselves most appropriately to a review of training needs because they represent an opportunity to consider a person's work in its entirety. Likewise, it is an occasion on which to consider the whole person – his/her strengths and weaknesses and his/her fit with the job.

An employee's first appraisal interview should occur within the first six months at the latest, and certainly before any probationary period expires. After that appraisals are normally held annually but may be held more frequently if it is important to monitor employee performance or if the organisation is changing rapidly and needs to reframe continuously its desired competences.

This session has already explained a lot of the preparation for the appraisal. In designing the job specification, the HRD will have reflected the future needs of the organisation (to the extent that they are known). These are key ingredients in identifying the criteria for the appraisal.

There is a further, crucial stage: the manager's assessment. The manager must take time to reflect on the evidence to ensure that he/she is forming a fair and objective view of the employee. He/she will be expected (rightly) to justify any adverse or positive comments made during the interview and so gathering the evidence is an important component of this stage.

6.5.1 Appraisal interview

There are eight steps in conducting an appraisal interview, as follows.

1. The appraisal interview should begin with a brief progress report, looking back in a positive way to the last appraisal interview.
2. The appraisee should give his/her views about what he/she thinks have been the most significant successes and failures since the last appraisal.
3. A discussion about how the appraisee sees these successes and failures should take place.
4. The appraisee should give his/her views on how he/she could be more effective and what the manager's contribution to this will be.
5. Time should be spent identifying and agreeing on how future work will be approached.
6. Priorities (targets) for important tasks up to the next appraisal interview should be agreed and set.

7   Any training and development needs should be discussed and the necessary plans made.

8   The outcomes of the interview should be agreed.

It is inevitable that there will be at least one part of the job that requires personal improvement and the appraisee may be relieved to talk about it. It is not uncommon in appraisals for the appraisee's judgement to be more harsh than the appraiser's. Constraints that affect the ability to perform should be examined. It may be simply that too much is required – a not unusual circumstance in an ever-changing organisational environment.

There should be time at the end of the appraisal interview to allow employees to raise any other issues. The appraiser(s) should listen carefully before summarising what has been discussed, what has been agreed and what action, if any, needs to be taken as a result of the discussion. Both appraiser and appraisee need to agree objectives for the period between this appraisal and the next one. Once agreed, these objectives will form the basis for the next appraisal. The appraiser will normally write a report of the appraisal meeting including the objectives for the next period. The appraisee will sign it once he/she is happy that the report accurately covers what was discussed.

Many organisations use an appraisal form, which the employee completes prior to the appraisal interview. Such a form might include:

- a brief report on progress since the last appraisal
- the employee's view on what have been his/her most significant achievements and failures during that period
- the employee's career aspirations
- the employee's training and development needs
- the employee's views on how he/she might perform the job more effectively
- specific help the employee might need from the line manager.

This rating method was first established in the British Civil Service.

The generally recommended pattern is to encourage the appraisee to undertake self-appraisal. To do this, an employee may be required to list the key areas that are critical to the job, rating his/her performance over the past six months in relation to each key area. This, as you may well realise, is a tricky task to undertake. Each one of us may believe that our work is very good, or average, or outstanding, but dare we put it in writing? Perhaps not!

A more effective procedure requires answering specific questions in two categories (as set out in the following table) that more accurately describe who the appraisee is, what they are doing and what they need to do in order to do it better.

Performance improvement	Career development
What do you see as your priority tasks for the next year?	What are your present career ambitions? Specify action that would provide for your longer term development.
Are there any constraints or problems that adversely affect your performance? How could these be diminished?	Which other jobs do you feel you could undertake as an alternative to your own, not necessarily in your own department or division?
What do you consider are your major strengths?	Are your abilities being fully utilised in your present job?
What development or training would be helpful for you in your present job?	Any further information you feel is relevant?

6.5.2 Appraising performance

This is a more realistic and positive way of appraising performance. It can also be an extremely effective way of prompting consideration of the resources, support, training and development that will help employees to achieve their maximum potential. Having completed such a task as answering these questions, it can then be beneficial to have an appraisal interview. This may be conducted by the line manager or the line manager's manager. In larger organisations a member of staff from the HRD may also be present.

After the interview is completed it is important to record everything that has been agreed. This should be signed off by both the manager and the appraisee to ensure that they both fully understood the discussion. One or both parties can misinterpret something and completing a record and signing it gives the chance to correct any misunderstanding.

The report acts as a record and also as a framework for the actions that have been agreed by both parties. The line manager may have agreed to certain training requirements while the appraisee may have made a commitment to carry out certain actions.

Both parties need to ensure that they follow through on the agreed action plans. This should be monitored and reviewed periodically. The action plan should specify when reviews will take place.

6.6 Development and delivery of the training and development programme

You should now have a clear understanding of how to establish what training an individual needs. This section describes how the training could be delivered.

6.6.1 Developing employees' skills

An induction programme is usually the first introduction to training and development that an employee will experience. Depending upon the size of the organisation, it is usually the line manager's job to work out an induction programme for the new member of staff, in conjunction with the training manager if there is one. The purpose of the induction programme is to introduce any new recruits to key people in the organisation with whom they will need to communicate in order to do their job, to show them the tasks for which they are responsible and where to go for information, resources and help.

Managers may decide to enable employees to develop their skills further by means of courses which may be run by external consultants. Other ways of developing staff are in-house development, coaching and mentoring.

In-house development

'Don't worry about doing the right thing. There'll be plenty of time for that after you're fired, retired or reincarnated.'

There is a number of ways in which skills can be developed. Not all of these involve formal training.

It does not follow that in-house training is inferior in any way if compared with attending a course run by a party external to the organisation. There are many different types of in-house training, which are set out below.

Job rotation. This means encouraging members of a team to be able to work proficiently in each other's jobs, thus creating greater flexibility and skills within the team as a whole. Job rotation also helps people to appreciate just how difficult certain jobs really are.

Special assignments or projects. This means increasing the skills base of individuals by arranging supervised project work in preparation for greater responsibilities.

Action learning. This is where a group of individuals work on their own chosen problems, and also share advice and approaches to solving each other's problems. This type of training can be invaluable. Each person in turn describes to the group a work dilemma, which is causing upset in his/her department. The dilemma then becomes the group's problem, and each person in the group works on the problem in an attempt to find a solution. Because the person who described the problem is so close to it, he/she often cannot therefore find a way around it. The solution offered by the group might be simple, but effective.

In-house courses. These provide a means of conveying knowledge and skills to groups of individuals through trainers (either from within the organisation or from external providers who visit the organisation).

People may reach a stage in their careers when they are being considered for promotion to a role which will perhaps involve supervision of staff members. Two specific types of development that can be helpful to such an individual seeking promotion to a supervisory role are coaching and mentoring.

Coaching

Coaching is a way of transferring knowledge and skills from a more experienced person to a less experienced person. At all times, the following processes apply.

- The coach and the person being coached spend time together that is protected and uninterrupted. The first task is to define what needs to be done.
- The less experienced person may shadow the more experienced colleague, observing what is going on and asking questions.
- When the person being coached experiences a situation where advice is needed, the coach will ask questions, probing to see if the individual has thought about different possible choices or courses of action.
- New ideas might be offered, but individuals should be encouraged to 'talk through' their own solutions. The coach may then say: 'What might happen if you did that?' The consequences of actions are very important, especially when managing people and, more especially, when the manager is new to the role.

Mentoring

A similar activity to coaching is mentoring, although one of the fundamental differences is that a mentor should not be the individual's line manager. Mentors are people with responsibility for overseeing the development of others outside the normal manager–subordinate relationship. Mentors are often older, or at least considerably more experienced, than the individuals they are mentoring. They provide support, encouragement and opportunities for development, by acting as a 'sounding board' for ideas.

The skills and attributes of a mentor include the following.

- A strong motivation to assist in the development of others.
- Considerable and acknowledged experience in the skills being mentored.
- The ability to identify the strengths and weaknesses of the mentee (the person being mentored) and the ability to formulate developmental or remedial activities.
- The personal skills necessary to build a relationship with the mentee and with his/her line manager.

When your tutor first started work with The Open University, he/she will have had a mentor to help during the first presentation of the module on which he/she tutored students. The OU mentor would contact the new tutor to talk about how to support students and how to approach the first tutorial. The mentor would remain in contact for the first year until the new tutor became established. For example, marking TMAs can be quite daunting for a new tutor, even though guidelines are given by the Module Team Chair. The tutor and the mentor may decide to mark a few scripts together. This ensures that you, the student, will benefit from the knowledge of the experienced tutor which has been shared with the new recruit.

Summary

Training and development is a continuous process, with no definite end point. Increasingly, organisations are formulating policies to stimulate, manage and find sufficient resources for staff development as an essential element of their efforts to improve performance and effectiveness and to maximise opportunities for all.

Emphasis has been placed on each one of us – as employees – to contribute to our own development as well as to help our organisation to achieve the goals and objectives that it pursues.

SESSION 7 Recruitment and selection

Introduction

Upon completion of Session 7 you are expected to be able to:

- explain the importance of effective recruitment and selection for the organisation
- describe the recruitment and selection process, including the stages and the roles of the people involved in the process
- describe the methods through which organisations seek to meet their recruitment needs.

In the previous session the importance of people to an organisation was discussed and an approach to developing a flexible and high performing workforce described. There are significant advantages to organisations developing their existing workforce but occasionally people with specific skills that are not readily available within the existing workforce, or not available in sufficient quantity, are required. An organisation also needs new recruits to balance staff losses (through people changing jobs or through retirement) or to increase staffing levels to meet organisational goals. It follows, then, that a key activity in any organisation should be the recruitment and selection of staff.

When someone leaves a team, the temptation is to fill that vacancy quickly because the quantity of work generally does not reduce when a worker leaves. However, it is a good opportunity to stand back and consider, not just what the individual used to do in the team, but also what the team might be doing in the future. Should the new recruit have the same skills and behaviours as the previous post-holder? Is it a chance to appoint someone who has different skills and, at the same time, give the other team members the chance to develop their own skills by taking on new roles?

The chances are that, in many organisations, the job description of the person who has just left will be retrieved and will be used as the basis for recruitment. In more forward-looking organisations, the line manager will work with the HRD to develop a new job description that takes into consideration the business strategy for the next five years.

This session looks briefly at how recruitment and selection should be done. You may not be in a position at present to recruit staff yourself, so if this is the case, study this session from the perspective of a potential recruit. You may learn much about a future employer's willingness to invest in human resources by analysing that employer's approach to this key area of activity.

7.1 Effective recruitment

The process of recruitment has evolved considerably in the last few decades. When Fayol (about whom you will recall reading in Session 1) started writing on the theory of management, it was not unusual to obtain a job as a result of a personal recommendation from a friend, neighbour or relative who already had a job in a firm. In manufacturing industries and in small firms, it was believed that a person so recommended would remain loyal to the group and to the organisation. Any analysis of an individual's skills was perfunctory. For manual work the recommendation was probably enough to secure the job. Even for skilled or managerial work, say, that of an accountant, possessing the appropriate qualification proved that you were capable. The applicant might need a reference from any previous employer but that would say little, or nothing, about the individual's competence at the job, yet, once he/she got the job, it was often a job for life, irrespective of suitability.

How could the management or owners of these organisations know that they were recruiting people of the right calibre? It was largely luck and, of course, this was an age where poor performers could often lose themselves in large workforces and not come to anyone's attention!

Activity 7.1

Today, even small firms are likely to have a written recruitment policy. Write down three things it might cover.

Allow five minutes for this activity.

Feedback

You may have considered many things that could be included in a recruitment policy. Here are a few suggestions:

● a commitment to open, non-discriminatory recruitment

● a commitment to flexible and family-friendly employment facilitating recruitment of people with young families

● a minimum level of educational attainment for specific roles

● a required level of experience for specific roles

● a geographical range for recruitment facilitating recruitment without the need for relocation of the potential recruit.

Hopefully any other points that you came up with will be covered in more detail during this session.

The costs of recruiting even one employee are considerable, in terms of the internal time involved in creating the paperwork, examining the application forms, arranging interviews, deciding who will ask which questions during the interview and showing the candidates around part of the organisation. There are also the potentially high external costs of advertising the post.

However, the cost of a wrong decision can be even higher. Today, recruiting someone who does not fit with the organisation's needs is potentially very damaging to the ability of the business to meet its objectives. Organisations are run very leanly. Each member of staff is critical to the performance of the organisation and it takes time to recognise, and then (quite rightly) even more time to remove, a poorly selected individual. Figure 15 shows the steps in recruiting and selecting staff.

Recruitment and selection

Define job specification	Decide: recruit or promote?	Advertising	Selection	Follow up
Align requirements with strategy	Internal resources	Qualities of advertisement	Administration	References
Review job description	External resources	Choice of media	Filtering	Induction
Re-evaluate job specification	Timing		Evaluation	Training and Development
	Development		Selection	
	Innovation			

Evaluate process

Figure 15   A plan for managing recruitment and selection

7.2 Job analysis, description and specification

Understanding what you want to recruit someone to do seems an obvious first step, yet all too often organisations simply advertise to replace someone who has left the organisation. This is an ideal time to confirm that you understand the current competences needed. Job analysis (the development of a job description) was discussed in the last session. Do you recall the process involved?

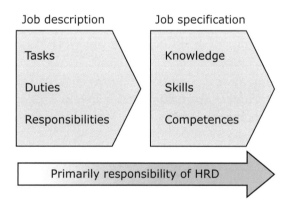

Job description	Job specification
Tasks	Knowledge
Duties	Skills
Responsibilities	Competences

Primarily responsibility of HRD

Figure 16   Job description and specification

Staff members in the HRD undertake an analysis of the job in order to define its tasks, duties and responsibilities. They then consider the knowledge, skills and competences needed for someone to perform the job well. You may also recall that it was suggested that part of the duties might be to provide flexibility to meet organisational change and to cover for colleagues and superiors during their absence. If the HRD is aware of the strategic direction of change within an organisation, there is the opportunity to 'fine tune' the tasks and duties to meet those changes. The knowledge, skills and competences will then also reflect the needs of the organisation to prepare its staff for future changes. In an ideal world, this analysis would be redone every time a vacancy occurs. Unfortunately, many organisations merely retrieve the job description used last time. We can help to avoid this by having a systematic approach to recruitment and selection.

7.3 Recruit or promote?

Most organisations will normally look first to promote someone into a vacancy provided that there is a suitable candidate. This can be important to the existing workforce even if they are not candidates for promotion as they can see that internal promotion is a possibility. This can be a powerful intrinsic motivator (you will recall these from Session 4). Conversely it can be very demotivating to see someone appointed from outside and take the job that you wanted, particularly if you then have to help that person to settle in. However, there can be lots of reasons why an external recruit may be preferable, as explained below.

Quality of the internal pool. Are there sufficient internal candidates with the appropriate competences for the job? By being methodical in the performance appraisal process, the HRD should be able to build an accurate picture of the internal labour pool.

Quality of the external pool. There may be more potential recruits with the appropriate competences outside the organisation than within it, especially if the job specification may require specialist skills.

Timing. How urgent is it to fill the role? However, an unsuitable internal recruit should not be chosen over an external one simply because it is urgent to fill the role.

Development. The opportunity to develop the internal pool by recruiting high calibre external candidates with a specific remit to introduce new skills across the workforce should not be overlooked.

Innovation. It can be advantageous to bring in skills and experiences from competitor firms. This is a key way by which an organisation learns.

7.4 Advertising

If an organisation decides to recruit from outside the organisation, it will need to attract as many suitable candidates as possible. To do this, it must advertise the vacancy. If the response is to be cost effective, it follows that the content of the advertisement should encourage suitable people to apply for the job. Likewise, it should discourage unsuitable candidates from applying. Much individual and organisational time can be wasted by having to sift through unsuitable applications and it is unfair to applicants to raise false expectations. All advertising should be checked carefully to ensure that it does not contravene local legislation. In most countries legislation has been enacted to prohibit discrimination.

Choice of media

The choice of media is critical to obtaining suitable candidates. You would not advertise in the financial press for florists. There may be some florists who read the financial press but most are not likely to do so. However, if you advertise in a trade magazine, then your readership will increase. Similarly, there is no point in a national advertising campaign to fill a local vacancy where there is an adequate pool of suitably skilled workers close to your site. The criteria that you might consider are set out below.

Geographic range. Do you need to advertise locally, nationally or internationally?

Nature of the vacancy. Are there any specialised skills or professional qualifications needed (such as an accounting qualification)?

Speed. Are you comfortable advertising in a monthly periodical or do you wish to advertise in a daily newspaper?

Cost. The national press is more expensive than the local newspaper. Cost will therefore play a part in the decision.

Having selected the media, which may include the company's website and use of recruitment agencies, you need to design the advertisement carefully. It should be concise and attractively presented: it does, after all, represent your organisation.

Nature of the advertisement

The advertisement should include the basic information appropriate to the nature of the vacancy, as itemised below.

- The name of the organisation is usually essential (although some advertisements for high profile roles will simply say 'for a FTSE 100 public company').

- The nature of the job and the key competences, together with any required academic or professional qualifications or experience needed.

- The main benefits and conditions of employment. Here you would include the information normal for the industry of the job role. Many more senior management roles will simply state that pay and conditions are competitive. This leaves room to negotiate the exact terms after the selection process is completed.

The advertisement also needs to include the application process. This can of itself introduce a degree of selection. An online application will tend to exclude anyone not comfortable with the Internet whereas a requirement to complete the application by hand can deter others.

However the applicant responds, an application form is generally a good idea as it can help considerably in the initial selection stages.

Activity 7.2 ....

There is a number of ways in which organisations may wish to receive applications for jobs. The way in which the applicant's information is provided to the organisation should conform with how the organisation wishes to receive it. Thus applicants may have to submit handwritten applications in some cases while, in other cases, they must submit an electronic application.

Consider the following approaches that could be adopted by an organisation seeking to fill a vacancy for a management accountant:

- sending a standard application form along with the job description

- asking applicants to e-mail a letter of application and curriculum vitae (CV).

From the perspective of the organisation, write down one advantage and one disadvantage for each of these methods.

Spend about five minutes on this activity.

Feedback ....

You may have thought of more than one example of each and, if you have done so, well done. Here are our thoughts.

Application form disadvantage. This may limit the scope of information that an applicant will provide and exclude mention of a useful competence that the organisation did not consider core to the job specification, but which may become important. For example, if the organisation has a subsidiary operation in say, Brazil, and the applicant used to live there, this may make it easier for the applicant to understand the culture behind the management accounting numbers being submitted to the parent company.

Application form advantage. Standardising the application form will simplify finding key pieces of information when sifting through a large number of applications.

CV disadvantage. By using e-mail the organisation may be excluding a range of applicants who may not have ready access to the Internet.

CV advantage. By using e-mail the organisation may be deliberately excluding applicants who are not familiar or comfortable with communicating via the Internet.

7.5 The selection process

Selection methods need to be cost effective and comply with relevant legislation.

Administration

Administration of recruitment needs to be managed effectively. Any HRD is likely to have a well organised clerical system for dealing with the paperwork that follows a recruitment campaign. Although this should be a straightforward, logical process, you may not be surprised to know that organisations sometimes get it wrong. Prospective applicants may telephone in response to an advertisement, only to find that no one at the switchboard knows about a job vacancy! This can be harmful for a firm's public image, making it even more difficult to recruit the right person for the job. Remember that candidates are also making choices – about whether they actually want to apply for the job. This makes it increasingly important for organisations to treat candidates in a sensitive and responsive manner.

Filtering

For some applications an organisation may be faced with hundreds of applications for one role. By designing the advertisement carefully, a degree of self-selection can be encouraged in the applicants. Hopefully those without the requisite skills will decide not to apply. Short-listing candidates is the first step in the selection process after applications are received.

Intuition must never be relied upon to select which candidates should be invited to interview. The skills highlighted in the job analysis can be used here to eliminate the less suitable candidates. If the application form has been carefully designed, then one or two key competences can quickly be identified for an initial filtering into possible and unsuitable candidates. This initial filtering will be carried out by the HRD. If the number of potential candidates is still too large, further required attributes (such as 'ability to drive' or 'residence location') may be added to the short-listing criteria.

Evaluation

Once the HRD has produced a short list of suitable candidates, this list is passed to the line manager who will be responsible for the individual who is eventually selected. The line manager will then review each of these candidates carefully. Some may be rejected at this stage or indeed, the line manager may ask to see a slightly wider selection if he/she feels that the short list does not provide sufficient candidates who are considered suitable. Throughout this review process the line manager should make careful notes of areas that he/she wants to explore with the candidate at an interview.

This evaluation is an important step, frequently overlooked by line managers. There is a real danger in holding any interviews without being thoroughly prepared. The line manager will need to probe the candidate on a number of areas in order to ensure that he/she is suitable for the role.

Selection

It is often said that many interviews are conducted by untrained personnel who fail to recognise the consequences of their decisions. What is even worse, many interviewers base their judgements on first impressions. The tone of a speaker's voice combined with non-verbal signals (facial expressions, posture and gestures) can have a strong influence on the opinion of the interviewer.

If you have ever been involved in interviewing applicants for a job, were you swayed by first impressions?

One method often used by interviewers is to rank candidates. This is understandable but could lead to selecting a candidate where none of them are truly suitable. To recruit the best person for the job, it is necessary to compare candidates, not against each other but against the job specification.

A selection interview aims to:

- explain the work of the organisation
- describe the job realistically
- find out whether a candidate will be suitable and elicit the qualities that he/she will bring
- set expectations on both sides
- enable the candidate to assess whether he/she wants the job.

A pre-interview tour of where the successful candidate will work is advantageous, both to the candidate and to the team who will be working with this person. Although the team would play no part in the selection process, it gives the interviewee the chance to ask questions and to see the people with whom they may be working.

7.5.1   The selection interview

Interviews need to be planned to enable the candidate and interviewer(s) to communicate effectively. The interviewer should be equipped with the following details/information.

> *Terms and conditions.* He/she should have full information on the job, the proposed wage or salary level and details of the conditions of employment.

The job (or person) specification. The interviewer should have a list of the attributes and characteristics required for the job, as well as the application form or letter in order to pinpoint items that he/she may want to find out more about during the interview.

A schedule of key questions. Many well prepared line managers will have a standard set of questions to which they add the questions that they noted during the evaluation of the application forms.

References or reports of candidate. The interviewer will need any references if these are going to be considered before or during the interview process or any special reports on the candidates if they are internal applicants.

If two or more people are conducting the interview, then the burden of information gathering and interview questioning can be shared. If this is the case, a plan must be drawn up beforehand so that each person on the interview panel knows exactly what he/she will say, ask and do.

Activity 7.3

What information does the candidate need from an interview? Try to think of an interview that you have attended. Write down at least four information needs you had when you arrived for the interview.

Allow five minutes for this activity.

Feedback

It is useful to think about the information that a candidate will need because the interviewer will need to have this information available. Here are some thoughts.

- The exact nature of the role, its full specification and the responsibilities that go along with it. For example, will these include late night working or weekend work?

- Some initial indication of the culture. Will a successful candidate be required to wear formal clothing or can he/she dress casually? Will he/she be working in isolation, in a small team or a large open workspace? The candidate is likely to form some opinions about the organisation's culture from observing the interviewer, the quality of the administration for the interview and the location of the interview, so it is important for the interviewer to pay attention to these details.

- The opportunities for development and advancement within the organisation.

- Every candidate will be interested in the terms of employment, such as salary and benefits, but these may not always be discussed in detail at the initial interview. The candidate may, however, wish to know the salary structure (such as whether it will be a basic wage plus bonus). The candidate may also be interested in issues connected with joining the organisation, such as whether there will be a relocation allowance or how quickly he/she might be required to start.

As you can see, there is a large range of issues to which a candidate may want answers and you could probably have thought of a lot more than four. By thinking carefully about what a candidate may ask, the interviewer should be better prepared for the interview.

The interview location

A suitable room is essential and it should be prepared in advance. Some interviews might benefit from the formality of an office while others might be better conducted in a more relaxed setting. A desk implies formality and places a barrier between the interviewers and the candidate. Adverse effects can also arise from such factors as seating the candidate on a low chair at a distance, placing them where the sun is in his/her eyes, or drinking tea while the candidate remains thirsty.

The interview plan

A structured interview, organised in a series of discrete units or areas of enquiry, each of which may be assessed separately, is much more likely to achieve its purpose than an unstructured interview. The plan should therefore provide a route through the interview.

The qualities and experience that candidates detailed on the application forms led to their selection for interview. Now it is time to look at the following three key questions.

Could the candidate do the job? Does he/she have the appropriate skills and intelligence? The questions asked should be open ones, for example: 'What does your present job involve?'. This allows the candidate to speak, and allows the interviewer to listen (watching for non-verbal signs) and to ask further questions about tasks and abilities in the candidate's job that will be required for the current position.

Would the candidate do the job? The candidate may well have the necessary skills, but may lack the motivation considered necessary. An effective question here might be: 'Can you tell us why you'd like to work for our firm?' (This is more polite than asking 'Why do you want to leave your current job?' and there is a good chance that the candidate – anticipating this question – will have a well thought out reply.)

Would the candidate fit in? Does he/she have the type of personal characteristics that could readily be accommodated by key colleagues within the department or the organisation as a whole? Careful questioning about people's leisure activities and hobbies can yield a lot of information which could give clues as to how well they might fit in. For example, what type of activities spark their enthusiasm? If sport, is this team sport or a lone sport or a mere observer of sport? Do other people select him/her for positions of responsibility outside the working environment?

It could be argued that placing too much emphasis on whether a person will fit in may eventually lead to stagnation if the selection process continues to produce only people who fit the organisational mould and appear to be 'one of us'. Also, if taken to an extreme, it could actually be discriminatory and so some organisations will not allow these kinds of questions to be asked.

Another technique is to devise a short scenario describing a tense situation from normal every day life in the area in which the candidate will work. The scenario is then explained to the candidate, asking: 'How would you deal with this if it happened to you?' This is, perhaps, the only type of question in the entire interview for which a candidate cannot prepare beforehand.

The purpose of the interview is to collect evidence, using eyes and ears, so that a choice can eventually be made. A practical target is to expect the candidate to talk for about 70 per cent of the time. If this is to be achieved, it is necessary to keep the candidate talking about the things that the panel needs to know. This means avoiding closed questions that can be answered with 'Yes', 'No' or 'Not really'. Most candidates will expect to be asked what special qualities they would bring to the organisation.

7.5.2   Other selection techniques

Selection testing

Some organisations use techniques such as psychometric testing to measure a candidate's intelligence and aptitude to carry out specific types of work. While these techniques can be very useful, they do have limitations. Usually they are designed to capture a discrete range of aptitudes such as intelligence, verbal reasoning and personality traits. The line manager should use them to supplement other selection techniques, not to replace them.

Another form of selection testing is to place the candidate in a mock work situation. Perhaps he/she will need to solve a problem that is likely to occur. This can be a very useful way of confirming that what the candidate tells you about his/her experience or training is accurate. However realistic the work situation that you create, nonetheless it will always be false. The candidate is likely to be nervous and his/her performance will possibly not be truly reflective of ability. Therefore, while useful, use of a mock work situation should also be used to supplement other selection techniques, not to replace them.

All tests may be subject to bias. Some candidates will have done many similar tests before, particularly psychometric tests, and be more competent at them than others. Thus the tests will not so usefully assess their underlying ability. Some other candidates may be using a second language, putting them at a disadvantage.

Assessment centres

It has become common for organisations that recruit a number of university graduates each year to ask the candidates to attend a day (or more) at an assessment centre. 'Assessment centres' provide highly structured testing and interviewing of the candidates. The technique is also commonly used for senior management appointments.

During the assessment candidates will:
- undertake role play exercises which test their ability to handle different work-related situations
- be given case studies with more time to complete them than is typical when they are given a short, mock work exercise in a normal selection process
- be expected to mix socially, perhaps over lunch or even dinner
- be interviewed by different people.

During the whole period the line manager (and probably a few colleagues) will observe the candidates. This extended process provides a much more detailed and reliable assessment of candidates but is expensive, both in management time and financially. It is therefore rarely used for middle management or non-management recruitment.

7.6 Follow-up

Once the successful candidate is chosen, a formal offer will be made. If not already done, the final terms and conditions will be negotiated and the offer made conditional sometimes on the outcome of a medical check-up and receipt of satisfactory references.

7.6.1 References

References can be useful, despite having some limitations. It would be foolish for a candidate to name a referee who was going to give a bad reference. Rather than asking candidates to include a reference or references with their application, some organisations prefer to ask applicants simply to supply the name of two referees who may be contacted. Once the short list has been drawn up, the referees for all short-listed candidates may be approached and asked for their opinion. Sometimes they are asked to make comments under specific headings. This avoids bland references that only highlight a candidate's positive qualities as seen by their referee. Sometimes the referees may be sent a questionnaire to fill in about the candidate. One referee is usually someone who can comment about a person's approach to work. This is normally the current employer. However, some candidates may not want their current employer approached until they have actually been offered a job.

There is also the issue of the point at which the references should be read during the selection process and also what is the real purpose of references. Some interview panels like to read the references along with the application form as part of the interview preparation. This allows them to check that what candidates have said about themselves is correct and to note down any points they want to follow up at interview. However, this would not be regarded as best practice, as there could be the danger that some comment in a reference might prejudice the interview panel, either in favour of or against a particular candidate. It would be unfair, for example, if a particularly fulsome reference for one candidate gave that person an undue advantage over another candidate whose referee had been less effusive.

For this reason, other interview panels prefer to open the references only once all the interviews for the post are over. Yet others do not look at the references until the panel has reached a decision about whom to appoint. In this case, the reference simply serves to confirm statements that the candidate has made about background and work experience. Sometimes references are not taken up until after the interviews are completed and in this case the candidate will be told that a job offer will be made following confirmation from referees.

7.6.2   Induction, training and development

No matter how competent the candidate is, he/she will need to undertake some formal induction and an initial training and development plan should be put in place (you will recall the processes around this from Session 6).

Activity 7.4

Imagine you are about to interview someone to do your present or previous job. Write down a list of the questions you would ask, and why you want to ask each question.

Allow about ten minutes for this activity.

Feedback

By now you should be thinking about the individual's competences for the role. You have done some work on your job descriptions and can refer to specific tasks and responsibilities that the candidate may need. Of course, the specifics must be individual to your job, but this activity should reinforce the need to prepare a good job description before embarking on a recruitment programme.

Summary

This session has presented guidance on the process of recruiting and selecting employees who will work together to achieve the objectives of the organisation. The cornerstone of the process is the compilation of an analysis of the tasks which, taken together, make up the job description and the job (or person) specification as discussed in Session 6. Appropriate methods of candidate selection and interview skills will help to ensure that the best person is chosen for the job as described.

Unit summary

Well done! You have now completed Unit 6 of B292 *Management accounting.*

During this unit you have explored a broad range of disciplines associated with management. You should now have a good understanding of the theory of management and leadership as well as how differing stakeholders and organisational culture can either assist or inhibit management action. You also explored the subject of motivating individuals within the organisation, considering how the individuals may fit into both formal and informal groups and how good managers might influence the effectiveness of such groups. Finally, the nature of formal training and development of the workforce within an organisation, and the recruitment and selection of people to join the workforce, were explored.

Before moving on to Unit 7, attempt the following self-assessed questions. Make sure that you check your answer to each question with the various sessions in this unit before moving on to the next question.

Self-assessed Questions

Question 1

Taylor and Mayo were both researching into the nature of management early in the twentieth century but drew significantly different conclusions about how to improve the efficiency of a workforce. In what way do they differ?

Suggested answer

Taylor worked extensively with the nascent Ford Motor Company automobile production business and focused on scientific management, which detailed each stage of production in an attempt to derive the most efficient production method. He argued that workers were reluctant to improve productivity and therefore efficiency would be achieved through detailing every operation workers must carry out, and then encouraging them to complete each operation as quickly as possible. Usually this 'encouragement' was achieved by introducing piece-work rates where employees were paid for the number of operations completed.

Mayo conducted research at the Western Electric Hawthorne plant (the Hawthorne experiments) where he monitored two groups of workers, each group isolated from the other. He altered the physical working conditions of one group and found that productivity was not dependent on improving or worsening the physical conditions, but was dependent on the act of altering conditions. He concluded that the simple action of management paying attention to the workforce encouraged higher productivity. Mayo's revolutionary concept was that social man responds to a humanistic approach to management and that work satisfaction is a vital ingredient in motivation. This is in stark contrast to Taylor's rational man who Taylor believed had no interest in the work itself and had to be induced to produce effectively.

Question 2

Why is it important for an organisation to understand who the stakeholders are?

Suggested answer

Although customers' needs are of critical importance, the expectation of other stakeholders must also be considered – particularly those who can exercise power/influence on the organisation if their expectations are not satisfied. It is particularly important to identify those stakeholders who have most power and need to be part of the decision process.

Question 3

Schein described the third level determinant of culture as assumptions. The existence of such assumptions makes it very difficult for a manager new to an organisation to change an organisation's culture. What are assumptions in this context and why do they make it difficult to change a culture?

Suggested answer

Schein discussed three determinants of culture. The most obvious (first level) determinant is the observable level which consists of behaviours, artefacts (organisational flags and symbols being key examples of artefacts) and attitudes. Because these are easily observed, they are comparatively easy for a new manager to identify and address.

The second level determinants are values and beliefs. These are not obvious to an outside observer but are known to people inside the organisational culture. As such they can be discussed and a new manager can learn them over time. Once they are known, it is possible, if challenging, to start to change them.

It is the third level determinant, assumptions, which are difficult to identify, because people inside a culture are often not aware of assumptions themselves. Assumptions are often subconscious beliefs. It might be that an assumption exists that only people who work late are really contributing to performance, or that people who dress formally are not prepared to get involved with the production line of a factory. Such assumptions may be true or false, but a new manager cannot address them until he/she is aware of them. This is why the third level determinant is the most difficult barrier to changing culture.

Question 4

Distinguish between intrinsic and extrinsic rewards.

Suggested answer

Maslow described a hierarchy of needs which postulates that, once an individual has sufficient resources to cover both physiological needs (food and shelter) and to provide a level of safety (for example, job security and a good pension arrangement), individuals become less motivated by these basic requirements and increasingly motivated by other factors such as social needs (building a network of friends and enjoying the job). Physiological needs and safety are normally provided by money and are called extrinsic rewards whereas non-financial rewards, often seen as more influential for individuals higher up Maslow's hierarchy, are called intrinsic. Intrinsic rewards include factors such as recognition of a job well done, good training programmes and development structures, and overall job satisfaction.

Question 5

Explain Tuckman's four stages of group evolution. A fifth stage has subsequently been added: what is it?

Suggested answer

Tuckman differentiated four stages of group formation:

- *forming* where each member of the group gets to know the other members, their abilities and allegiances
- *storming* where the group members test each other and settle into group roles
- *norming* where the group members settle down to their respective roles and set out group 'norms' to which they expect each member to adhere
- *performing* where they finally get on with the allocated tasks.

The fifth stage follows once the group's purpose has been achieved. This is referred to as 'adjourning'.

If a group has been particularly successful, its members will feel a strong affiliation to it, as they will have invested a huge amount of personal energy in the work of the group, identified with the group's goals and adopted group norms. For many people, working in a group can also help to fulfil strong social needs. When the group is disbanded these people feel a sense of loss. They need to be allowed the opportunity to 'mourn' the passing of the group. It has been found that, if this is denied, people are less willing to commit themselves in the same way to a new group, fearing the disbanding of the new group could bring the risk of similar distress in the future.

Question 6

In a well managed organisation it is essential to develop skills within the workforce. Two in-house methods of doing this involve job rotation and action learning. Explain and contrast these two methods and suggest some advantages and disadvantages of each.

Suggested answer

Job rotation is an excellent way of broadening the skills base in a workforce. Individuals swap jobs for a defined period giving each active exposure to the other role. There are clear advantages in improving flexibility and the ability to cover for sickness and other forms of leave. It also develops people to take over from other people when the latter choose to leave the organisation or are promoted. However, while the rotation is on-going, the organisation can expect lowered efficiency as people learn new tasks. Often surplus people are required within the workforce to permit job rotation to happen.

Action learning in the context of in-house development involves a group of people sharing work experiences and problems with the intention of helping each other to overcome the difficulties they each face. The advantage is that it brings people with different disciplines together to focus on problems, or even people with similar disciplines but who do not have similar mindsets about what is possible. A key disadvantage of this approach is gaining the commitment of each member of the group, which may be influenced by time pressures on them. Also, selecting a suitable group may be difficult and often involves the intervention of the line manager of the person with the problem.

Both approaches involve individuals experiencing issues outside their normal work roles but action learning does not take people away from their normal jobs and it is directed towards groups of people finding new solutions. The whole group learns from the experience.

References

Adair, J. (1973) *Action-centred Leadership*, London, McGraw-Hill Book Company (UK) Ltd.

Belbin, R.M. (1981) *Management Teams*, London, Butterworth-Heinemann.

Bennis, W. (1998) *On Becoming a Leader,* London, Arrow Books.

Blake, R. and Mouton, J.S. (1964) *The Managerial Grid: The Key to Leadership Excellence*, Houston, TX, Gulf Publishing Co.

BusinessDictionary [online], http://www.businessdictionary.com/ (Accessed 18 February 2011).

Drucker, P.F. (1977) *People and Performance: The Best of Peter Drucker on Management*, New York, Harper's College Press.

Fayol, H. (1949) *General and Industrial Management*, London, Pitman.

Fiedler, F.E. (1967) *Theory of Leadership Effectiveness*, New York and London, McGraw-Hill.

Handy, C. (1985) *Understanding Organizations* (3rd edn), Harmondsworth, Penguin Books.

Handy, C. (1993) *Understanding Organizations* (4th edn), Harmondsworth, Penguin Books.

Heifetz, R.A. (1994) *Leadership Without Easy Answers,* Cambridge, MA, Belknap Press.

Heifetz R.A. and Laurie, D.L. (1997) 'The work of leadership', *Harvard Business Review,* vol. 75, no. 1, pp. 124–34.

Herzberg, F. (1959) *The Motivation to Work*, New York, John Wiley and Sons.

Herzberg, F. Mausner, B. and Snyderman, B.B. (2005) *The Motivation to Work* (8th edn) New Brunswick, Transaction Publishers.

Johnson, G., Scholes, K. and Whittington, R. (2005) *Exploring Corporate Strategy* (7th edn), London, FT/Prentice Hall.

Johnson, L. (2009) 'Which stakeholder should get priority?' *Financial Times*, 23 December, online at http://www.ft.com/cms/s/0/027a6616-ef69-11de-86c4-00144feab49a.html?nclick_check=1 (Accessed 18 February 2011).

Kolb, D.A. (1984) *Experiential Learning: Experience as the Source of Learning and Development*, Englewood Cliff, NJ, Prentice Hall.

Kolb, D.A. and Fry, R. (1975) 'Towards an applied theory of experiential learning' in Cooper, C. (ed) *Theories of Group Processes*, pp. 33–58, London, John Wiley.

Kotter, J.P. (1988) *The Leadership Factor*, New York, Free Press.

Maslow, A.H. (1943) 'A theory of human motivation', *Psychological Review*, vol. 50, no. 4, pp. 370–96.

Mayo, E. (1946) *The Human Problems of an Industrial Civilization*, Boston, MA, Harvard University.

McGregor, D. (1960) *The Human Side of Enterprise*, New York and London, McGraw-Hill.

Mendelow, A. (1991) 'Stakeholder mapping: the power/interest matrix', *Proceedings of the 2nd International Conference on Information Systems*, Cambridge, MA.

Mintzberg, H. (1980) *The Nature of Managerial Work*, London, Prentice Hall.

Mumford, A. (1996) 'Effective learners in action learning sets', *Employee Counselling Today, The Journal of Workplace Learning*, vol. 8, no. 6, pp. 3–10.

Peters, T.J. and Waterman, R.H. (1982) *In Search of Excellence: Lessons From America's Best Run Companies*, New York, Harper & Row.

Porter, L.W. and Lawler, E.E. (1968) *Managerial Attitudes and Performance*, Homewood, IL, Irwin.

Schein, E.H. (1970) *Organizational Psychology* (2nd edn), Englewood Cliffs, NJ, Prentice Hall.

Schein, E.H. (1985) *Organizational Culture and Leadership: a Dynamic View*, San Francisco, CA, Jossey-Bass.

Smith, A. (1776) *An Enquiry into the Nature and Causes of the Wealth of Nations*, Oxford, Clarendon Press (1976 edition).

Tannenbaum, R. and Schmidt, W. (1958) 'How to choose a leadership pattern', *Harvard Business Review*, vol. 36, no. 2, pp. 95–101.

Taylor, F.W. (1911) *The Principles of Scientific Management*, New York and London, Harper and Brothers.

Tuckman, B.W. (1965) 'Developmental sequence in small groups', *Psychological Bulletin*, vol. 63, no. 6, pp. 384–99.

Vroom, V.H. (1964) *Work and Motivation*, New York, Wiley.

Acknowledgements

Grateful acknowledgement is made to the following sources:

Text

Page 12: Taken from: www.provenmodels.com. Mintzberg, H. (1973) *Leadership and Management and Personnel Management.* Reproduced by permission.

Page 26: Johnson, L. (2009) 'Which stakeholder should get priority', *The Financial Times*, December 23, 2009. © Luke Johnson.

Figures

Figures 2 and 3: www.provenmodels.com. Mintzberg, H. (1973) *Leadership and Management* and *Personnel Management.*

Figure 4: Blake, R. and Mouton, J. (1964) *The Managerial Grid,* © 1964, Gulf Publishing Company.

Figure 7: Adapted from: Mendelow, A. (1991) *Proceedings of the Second International Conference on Information Systems*, 1991, Cambridge, MA.

Figure 8: Schein, Edgar H. (1985) *Organizational Culture and Leadership: A Dynamic View*, Jossey-Bass Inc.

Figure 13: Kolb, D.A. (1984) *Experiential Learning: Experience as the Source of Learning and Development*, Englewood Cliff, NJ, Prentice Hall.

Styles, Lawrence Erlbaum Associates.

Illustrations

Pages 8, 15, 46, 52, 60, 66, 75 and 92: © Cartoonstock.com.